Villages of France

Villages of France

Text by Joanna Sullam

Photographs by Charlie Waite

Foreword by John Ardagh

RIZZOLI
NEW YORK

For Rex and Jessamy

Text and photographs copyright © Charlie Waite 1988
Foreword copyright © John Ardagh 1988

First published in the United States of America in 1988 by
Rizzoli International Publications, Inc.
597 Fifth Avenue, New York, NY 10017
First published in 1988 by
George Weidenfeld & Nicolson Ltd

Library of Congress Cataloging-in-Publication Data
Sullam, Joanna.
The villages of France.
1. France – Description and travel – 1975 –
2. France – Description and travel – 1975 – Views.
3. Villages – France – Pictorial works.   I. Waite, Charlie.
II. Title.
DC29.3.S85 1988   944'.009734   87–43261
ISBN 0–8478–0927–7

Designed by Joy FitzSimmons
Colour separations by Newsele Litho Ltd
Filmset by Deltatype Ltd, Ellesmere Port
Printed and bound in Italy by L.E.G.O., Vicenza

Half-title page Salers, Cantal
Title page Saint-Cirq-Lapopie, Lot

Note: Villages in the book are arranged alphabetically.
The name of each village is followed by its *département*.

Contents

Foreword

Brantes, Vaucluse

From the tiny village of Brantes –
it has less than 100 inhabitants –
you can climb to the top of Mt
Ventoux or opt for the steep road
journey across the southern face,
though for at least six months of
the year the mountain is
snow-covered. It was here that
the great French botanist and
writer J.- H. Fabre identified
species of plants native to the far
north of Europe, such as the
Iceland poppy and the
Spitzbergen saxifrage.
Well-restored remnants of
fortifications round the upper
tiers of the village are a reminder
that it lies in what was once
frontier land between the duchy
of Provence and the kingdom of
France.

France today may be as modern-minded an industrial nation as any in Europe, but it still draws much of its secret strength from its ancient rural heritage. Not only does its richly varied agriculture still play a vital role in the economy, but the urban French remain proudly aware of their rural roots and attachments. Scratch a Parisian and you may well find the son of a Breton or Auvergnat peasant. The new high-rise estates in the surburbs of cities are full of recent emigrants from the depopulating villages of the vast and lovely hinterland, and many of them still return to their origins for holidays or weekends, to visit old Tante Louise in her quaint cottage or to deck out the disused family farmstead as a second home. Links between town and country thus remain remarkably close.

The essence of this old rural France is the panoply of villages, 30,000 in number (hamlets excluded), that stud the landscape. Their variety of visual and architectural styles is amazing – a delight for the visitor touring from region to region. For Frenchness wears not one but a hundred faces. And one reason for this rich diversity is that France is the only country that belongs both to north and to south Europe. The grey granite cottages of Celtic Brittany, austere but dignified, with elaborate stone carvings in their churchyards, are in another civilization from the Mediterranean world of Provence or Languedoc, where walled red-roofed villages cling to hilltops and old men play *boules* in shady squares. And in between these two extremes are many other local styles, dictated very often by the climate or by past availability of building materials – the half-timbered façades of cider-growing Normandy, repeated in a different form in wine-growing Alsace; the Alpine chalets of Savoy; the handsome low brick farmhouses of the Sologne woodlands; the galleried houses of Burgundy *vignerons* where the cellar is the main room; the stark, squat buildings of upland Auvergne, long a very poor area, where the dark slate roofs slope steeply to avoid damage from heavy snowfalls; and in contrast, the cheerful flower-decked red-and-white villages of the Basque country.

Despite dramatic post-war economic and social change, many of these old villages of France have retained their picturesque charm and their historic physical appearance to a surprising

degree. Concrete eyesores may have arisen along parts of the coastline of France and on the edges of many towns: but the deep countryside remains largely unspoilt, and here many old buildings are now being lovingly restored.

But this does not mean that rural France has become some kind of vast Red Indian reservation, untouched by a modern way of life. On the contrary: its physical continuity is all the more remarkable in view of the fact that the social make-up, the economy and even the lifestyles of these villages have all altered radically during the past forty years. For long centuries, relatively little had changed: in the 1920s and 1930s, writers were still depicting a peasant society that was anchored in a way of life and a structure dating back to the Middle Ages. Most ploughing was still done by oxen rather than by tractor. Most farmland was split up into tiny uneconomic smallholdings where the peasants lived in bitter poverty, ignored and despised by the rest of the nation. They were hardly yet touched by modern entertainments, so they made their own: on winter evenings they would gather round the hearth to tell folk-tales or sing the local songs, often in dialect, and in summer they would put on traditional costumes for village fêtes and folk-dances, to the tune of the old country instruments such as the *cornemuse, vielle* or *galoubet.*

Since the last war, for better or for worse – and I personally believe it has been largely for the better – various modern influences have totally transformed French agriculture and with it the lives of the farmers and villagers. Farm mechanization has caused more than six million people to move off the land and seek jobs in the towns, and farming's share of France's active population has dropped from thirty-five to under eight per cent and is falling still. Those who remain behind now have much larger farms and are far more prosperous: they have lost the old mentality of the *paysan* and have become more like small businessmen, as in Britain, obsessed by modern techniques of production and marketing. Thus the old gulf between town and country has narrowed.

Many smaller villages are now crumbling or abandoned, or are lived in by a few elderly people. Many thousands of local churches, cafés, shops and schools have closed. The remaining rural population is tending to regroup in the larger villages on main routes, and these by contrast are now livelier than ever, with many of the amenities of modern towns. Here the villagers have been adopting the tastes, dress and lifestyles of townsfolk. The old local languages such as Breton and Occitan are fast disappearing from daily use, as the older people die. The younger women wear jeans, not smocks. The colourful local costumes are seldom seen except sometimes at a festival. And at a village fête the dance music is today far less likely to come from a *vielle* or *tambourin* than from some local rock or pop group.

French rural life is today being given a powerful new shot in the arm by the arrival of sophisticated newcomers from the towns, who come not to do farming – that no longer offers outlets – but for other activities. This is a newer trend than the postwar rural exodus, and I see it as offering great hope for the future. These invaders, mostly middle class, are of two main kinds. First, there are those who simply want a second home for holidays and weekends, or who come to retire. Since abandoned farmsteads and cottages are so ubiquitous, such properties are not hard to acquire quite cheaply – and France easily holds the world record for ownership of *résidences secondaires*. Secondly, and more significant, there are those who want to transfer their main work activity from the hectic city to the quiet countryside. It is not easy to do this in isolation: but if just a few pioneers come, then others follow, so that little by little a whole new vibrant village community is formed. Not only have many thousands of artists, writers, craftsmen and other self-employed people settled in the pleasanter villages, in regions such as Provence, but some entrepreneurs have found that it is perfectly feasible to set up a small modern factory in some hamlet where surplus farm labour is plentiful and costs are far lower than in a city. Just two miles from the Berry village where Alain-Fournier set *Le Grand Meaulnes*, I found a thriving little electronics plant in a converted cowshed – one example among hundreds.

These varied newcomers, like the leisure-seekers and the professionals, are often fired with a sense of concern for rural environment and a desire to help revive village life. Much of the recent careful restoration of old country buildings has been due to *their* efforts and to the money and taste that they have lavished on the conversion of their homes, not only in the fashionable show-villages of Provence but in many other parts of France. If so many villages today look neatly groomed and aesthetically preserved, it is due much more to these immigrants than to the old local peasantry.

Thus the postwar rural revolution in France has finally come full circle. First one generation left the farms and villages for the towns; now a newer generation from the towns is seeking a return to the rural heritage. By an odd paradox, it is these modern urban émigrés, many the children or grandchildren of peasants, who are the surest guarantors of the future of French rural tradition and of the glories of French villages.

Introduction

Sablet, Vaucluse

Like Séguret, Sablet belongs to the string of villages which line the western slopes of the Dentelles de Montmirail, south of Vaison-la-Romaine. From Sablet, the Dentelles are a hard, white and brittle-looking crest of rocks breaking the skyline to the east. Each of these villages is surrounded by its own small, privately owned vineyards, producing highly individual and delicious wines, from the heady Gigondas to the fragrant sweet dessert wine Rasteau and the subtle Vacqueras, an elegant relative of Châteauneuf-du-Pape. If Vaison-la-Romaine and its spectacular Roman excavations form a cultural background to these villages, it is Carpentras, a few miles to the south, that provides hard-nosed business sense and an efficient network of transport to move the valuable early crops of cherries, melons and strawberries, and later lavender, to destinations all over Europe.

Many of France's oldest villages have their origins buried in the Dark Ages, long before the *hexagone* of France was crystallized politically, when the land was inhabited by several different races. Each left its mark: the great thumbprints of the Roman occupation – aqueducts, paved roads, amphitheatres – stand out clearly among less grandiose legacies, but even before them Greek explorers and invaders from across the Mediterranean had settled along the south coast, bringing with them the olive tree, the cypress, the rose (which has given Grasse its world-renowned perfume industry) and the idea of commerce. The Celts had already made incursions into France, travelling down the valleys of the Rhine and Rhône from central Europe, to reach as far as Italy and Spain. These *Galli (Gaulois)*, as the Romans called them, settled into tribal villages built of mud, wood and straw, where they lived as hunters with some domestic livestock. The villages were probably surrounded by a deep ditch surmounted by a wooden stockade, or a series of ditches round a hill, like Iron Age hill forts. Defences were vital for security, for Celtic tribes, or clans, were constantly at war stealing each other's livestock, abducting each other's women and killing each other's men in their efforts to increase their territory. It was impossible for a people so at odds with itself to survive independently for long, especially with the long arm of Rome reaching out for new additions to its Empire. In about 50 BC, not without a struggle, this land of Celts became a Roman province named Gallia (Gaul), and remained so for almost five hundred years.

The Roman occupation brought a new and rather pleasant quality of life to Gaul. The Romans not only improved roads and housing and knew how to exploit the native talent for agriculture, they also introduced a sophisticated way of life and a highly developed culture. They gave the different tribes of Gaul a geographical unity which brought peace and prosperity in its wake: Roman roads made communication easier and Roman law gave individuals security without, in theory, their having to fight for it. The assimilation of the Celtic tribes was more or less complete. Many Gauls were endowed with the title 'Roman citizen', though others were not so ready to accept the new order. The peasant farmers, faithful to their pagan gods, were wary of

the new Roman idols: they were to be wooed by another faith from the East.

In the first century AD evangelists from the eastern Mediterranean landed on the southern shores of France preaching Christianity, and during the next three hundred years, despite persecution, bloodshed and martyrdom, their influence crept slowly northwards, helping to establish the Christian church as a separate corporate body which anyone who dared to could join. The tidy and subdued pattern of life under the Romans was soon to disappear as the Empire fell prey to waves of barbarian invaders. By the end of the third century the Romans found themselves unable to protect Gaul's frontiers for lack of troops. The mercenaries they enlisted, paid for by extra taxes levied on the people, were members of the very tribes from whom Gaul was attempting to protect itself: Visigoths, Burgundians, Alamans and Franks, they formed themselves into marauding bands which attacked Gallic towns and villages and either made off with their booty or settled down to the business of creating their own small kingdoms. In time, as a natural consequence of intermarriage and commerce, they became accepted as citizens of Gaul, but the process of assimilation was bloody and violent. Saint-Bertrand-de-Comminges, or Lugdunum Convenarum, was a town with a population of sixty thousand. It was here, in the foothills of the Pyrenees, that Herod and his wife were exiled by the Emperor Caligula shortly after the crucifixion of Jesus. Its baths, theatre, forum and aqueduct, together with all the other ingredients of a well-run Roman town, were destroyed by the barbarians. Only a small nucleus of villagers managed to survive and keep the community alive, and in the twelfth century it flowered again.

Although the order of municipal life did not disappear at once, the overall fabric of Roman administration began to crumble, and Gaul once again became a patchwork of separate barbarian kingdoms. The ruler of one of these, Clovis, King of the Franks, who had occupied northern Gaul, was by far the most powerful. Although he was a Christian, under his rule and that of his forever feuding descendants, the Merovingian or 'long-haired' kings, life for the peasantry was black indeed. The king would move from one settlement to another, taking his court with him and claiming food, clothing, jewellery and even women as his right. For these poor farmers the only refuge, spiritual and physical, was the church, particularly the monasteries which were beginning to appear all over France. They became Christians almost by default, needing the security that only the monasteries could give them, and the abbots and abbesses were only too pleased to welcome new recruits, and therefore more hands to the plough. One of the villages in this book, Sainte-Enimie, has its roots in that era, when Enimie, sister of King

Barfleur, Manche

The sea-front at Barfleur must have heard many a valedictory prayer offered for those lost at sea. The waters are shallow and the currents swift round this coastline; it was from the small harbour that in 1180 Prince William, the son and heir of Henry I of England, sailed in the White Ship and was drowned when she struck a rock and sank with all hands. Earlier, in 1066, Duke William of Normandy set sail for England and a new kingdom from this very spot. Rue St Thomas, the main street, is lined with seventeenth- and eighteenth-century houses whose clean lines display the instinctive ability of the Normandy architect to marry buildings and their locations harmoniously. The graceful granite façades and the blue-grey roofs were the inspiration of the painter Paul Signac (1863–1935) who lived near the church, and in the early years of Impressionism this entire coastline and its luminous sky were painted time and again by Monet, Sisley, Cézanne and their contemporaries.

Dagobert, founded a monastery in a remote part of the Tarn gorges after she had been miraculously cured of leprosy.

Meanwhile, from across the Mediterranean came the threat that might topple the church, the one force for stability in the land. With the death in AD 632 of Muhammad the armies of Islam had enveloped the eastern Mediterranean coast and the body of Spain. By the early eighth century southern France (the name provided by Clovis) was under their control, and this was not a people who could be assimilated into the country as the Celts, Romans and even the barbarians had been. In the south, those peasants who could moved to rocky, inaccessible spots like Peillon, Eze and Lucéram. Other villages were simply taken over by the Saracens, and in one or two, for instance Balazuc on the River Ardèche, it is claimed that traces of Saracen blood survive in the dark skin and crinkled hair of some local people. But the Saracens left behind more than this: many features of southern France that foreigners find so attractive are of Moorish origin, such as village architecture, clay pots and jars, even saffron-coloured *bouillabaisse* and pancakes of buckwheat or *sarrasin*.

For two centuries the southern half of France was prey to Saracen incursions from Spain and along its vulnerable Mediterranean coastline. But among the little kingdoms in the north, the strong and influential family of Pépin was producing a series of leaders of whom Charlemagne was to be the greatest. His forebears had already established a strong alliance with Rome, and when Charlemagne visited Pope Adrian there in AD 774, he evolved a long-term plan to chase all pagans out of France, and to strengthen its borders and if possible extend them. At this time, rural communities centred on a seigneur, whose estates – including everything on the land, including people – might have been awarded to him by the king for military services. Other seigneurs were simply powerful lords who felt they owed allegiance to no one; and all treated their tenants as they chose. When Charlemagne died it seemed that anarchy and poverty would drag France back to its dark tribal beginnings; but the church, which already had a strong hold, and a loose but just workable form of local government, based on the remnants of the Roman administrative and legal system, combined to establish the basis of feudalism and feudal rights.

Some domains were quite small, and the village was simply a collection of huts near the seigneur's house; others contained several villages, each run by the seigneur's bailiff. The Seigneurie of Cardaillac, in the Lot, for example, possessed lands that took well over a day to cross. These broad territories encompassed rivers and mountains, fertile valleys and high bleak plateaux. Among the tenants were probably some who were descended from Roman slaves

Autoire, Lot

Autoire lies in a valley that splits an amphitheatre of cliffs beyond whose heights the bare Causse de Gramat stretches away. The River Autoire emerges from the rock just above the village and gushes out in a spectacular cascade before joining the River Bave and then the Dordogne.

The small fortified thirteenth-century church is a reminder that Autoire once controlled the steep pass that led from St-Céré on the plain to Padirac on the Causse de Gramat; there is a ruined stronghold pinned dizzily to the cliffs above the village known locally as the Château des Anglais. Similar ruins are dotted about south-west France and nobody knows who built them, though they probably date from long before the English set foot in the land.

who, having outlived their usefulness had been loaned a plot of land to cultivate, and others who were perhaps independent smallholders looking for security. Tenants could not consider themselves free: the seigneur might demand as many as three days' work a week or a percentage of their crops, or both, and more at harvest-time. On monastic land much the same rules applied. They had the right to use common pasture and woodland, though the ever unpopular bailiff was at pains to see these were not wrongly or wastefully exploited, and in return for their labours received three essentials: a position of sorts in a social order, protection from outside aggressors, and freedom from the threat of starvation, for in a year of poor harvests it would not be in the seigneur's interests to allow his tenants to starve to death while he grew fat on the stores in his barns. Manpower was his greatest asset and must be cultivated.

None the less, the village huts were primitive: one room, a floor of beaten earth, a door kept open so that the fire would draw, chickens wandering in and out, the stench of an oozing manure heap. Nor was a day's labour productive by today's standards, even on the great monastic farms, because there were so few good tools. Metal was used mainly for weapons, and apart from a few axe-heads, sickles and scythes, most tools were made of wood, their edges heated and hardened by fire. The forest had to be kept at bay, especially in the north, and the cleared ground was sown with different cereals depending on the climate. The yields were almost always poor and some of the grain had to be kept back to feed the working animals and for the next sowing. The rest was milled into a coarse flour for bread, the basis of the village diet (peasants tasted meat three or four times a year at most). If they had space, villagers would plant and tend a small vineyard, for wine was considered beneficial to the health.

Feudalism is a broad term, and the social systems it encompasses had no clear beginnings or endings. Some aspects of feudalism survived in France right up to the beginning of the Revolution in 1789, but periodically the system was nudged in new directions by developments in the social or economic spheres, in particular the tremendous progress in agricultural techniques in the twelfth century. Peasants learned how to harness the power of rivers and streams effectively, with the result that flour-mills proliferated, and nobody was obliged to use the seigneur's. The same power source was adapted to machines for making cloth and working metal, and windmills began to appear on the skyline, especially in Normandy. Now oxen were yoked in groups of six or eight to draw the much heavier but more efficient ploughs made by the village blacksmith, one of a new class of specialized craftsmen who began to appear in the community. If the peasants found they had more time to themselves, the seigneur's need for

manpower was greatly reduced. Tenants were now in a position to earn money, and began to pay their 'rent' in cash, not labour. They could now choose whether to learn a trade, to remain farmers, or even to live elsewhere, for monasteries were offering attractive terms to anyone who cared to found new villages on monastic land. A class of itinerant merchants emerged, moving from village to village, who encouraged the growth of what we might nowadays describe as trade fairs: exciting and colourful gatherings once or twice a year where information as well as goods was exchanged, and which helped villages to grow into towns. Bargemon in Provence, for example, became a market centre, as did the villages on the rich alluvial plains to the east of the Dôme volcanoes and those standing on the crossroads of the pilgrim routes to Santiago de Compostela, Rome and Palestine. As a result of these radical changes the quality of life in rural communities improved so dramatically that between the eleventh and thirteenth centuries the population is said to have trebled.

The North

Over the next two centuries, through periods of plague, war and famine, the villages attained a shape which in many cases remains unchanged today. It was largely dictated by the farming methods of the peasants, which in turn were governed by the nature of the land. In north-western France, Brittany and parts of Normandy, farmland was called *bocage*, a Norman word describing small fields, ditched and hedged or bordered by rows of trees. The lanes, hidden deep between the fields, formed the arteries of a rural community where farms were scattered over a wide area with no focal point. The farms and outbuildings, with their small but hierarchical communities of peasants, were like small hamlets, having no church, and were attached to the nearest large town or *bourg*, where the church claimed its due tithes. These isolated farmers would have had little experience of the sociability that develops in the close-knit structure of a real village.

In the north and east, beyond Paris, and as far south and east as the borders of the Bresse and the Jura, the land, once cleared of forest, was farmed in long regular strips with no enclosures, in a system known as 'open-field' farming. Crops were rotated every three years, and villagers always had the use of a plot or strip lying in each of three main sections. The village houses tended to be grouped tightly together, and only the châtelain and the church were allowed to

enclose land. Cattle were usually herded collectively and stabled in communal stables at one end of the main street.

Another type of village adapted itself to the vine-covered hills of Alsace and the Vosges. Here it was unthinkable to let buildings trespass on precious soil, so villages tended to be strung out in a long line, either in a fold of land where the soil was considered poor, or just below the tree-line, with the vineyards spread out below, or along the main highway. At harvest-time tumbrils overflowing with grapes rattled past the timber-framed houses, jostling with local traffic and long-distance travellers, as they made their way to the waiting wine-presses in the cellars.

Gordes, Vaucluse

In the sixteenth and seventeenth centuries Gordes was a wealthy and animated community famous for its tanneries and silk-weaving industry. Cloth and leather merchants gathered to trade in the main square by the Renaissance château. A twelfth-century fortress stood on this site and the medieval village grew from here.

Drawings and illuminations of the period show the house of the lowliest peasant still dismally rudimentary, though there may have been a proper chimney, and even an outside staircase so that the family could live separately from the animals. In the upper room there would be a table, a few stools and a bed, shared by as many as could squeeze in. Other villagers, more elevated in the complex peasant hierarchy, lived in quite substantial homes with two upper storeys and more than one bedroom. They wielded influence in the nearest town, and, surest sign of prosperity, controlled a good deal of land and the animals with which to work it. They could employ the lowest class of labourers to do the heavy work, and indeed the latter relied on this employment, together with collecting and selling or swapping nature's produce and the odd bit of poaching to keep body and soul together. The alternative was almost certainly vagrancy and starvation.

Between the comfortably prosperous villagers and the very poor lay the households most familiar from school history books. Their houses were built of stone or timber and daub, depending on the materials available, and had windows and some form of thatched roof weighted with stones. Parts of the house were set aside for different domestic functions, so there was a kitchen area in the main room, a separate bedroom and a hayloft, while outbuildings housed pigs, sheep, hens and grain. Owning a dovecot was at first the prerogative of the seigneur, who used the droppings as fertilizer, but later the wealthier peasants also added them to their houses or, particularly in the south-west, built free-standing ones. None of these peasants was yet a landowner, and they were all bound to pay seigneurial and church taxes. At the heart of the village stood the church, often the only stone building, with the market place, the tavern and the fountain, if there was one, in front of it. If the village was lucky enough to have a central source of water there would also be a *lavoir* where the women gathered to wash their linen and to gossip. The communal oven was usually in the main square, and some old people

can still remember running as children down to the oven with a prepared dish to be baked, and running back home with it, hot and steaming, an hour or two later.

These different meeting places were essential to village life, and since everyone also attended church on Sundays, there was a regular exchange of information. There was constant movement between the houses, the fields, the livestock, the church and the all-important common land as the villagers went about their business. In about 1400 the Limbourg brothers were commissioned by the Duke of Berry to paint calendar scenes for each month of the year. These remarkable pictures, *Les Très Riches Heures du Duc de Berry*, show the villagers, men and women alike, going about their daily tasks through all the seasons. We see the farm in bitter midwinter, with its wattle enclosure, a wattle pen for the sheep and even a wattle chimney with a feather of smoke in the cold air. The mistress of the house warms her feet close to the fire, while two more humble people, perhaps servants, sit behind her with their coarse tunics pulled above their knees, hoping for some warmth. Outside a man hurries past a row of snow-covered beehives, while a younger man chops firewood and yet another drives a laden donkey to the village in the distance. The church spire rises above the huddle of houses, and the walls of a castle are just visible on a hill beyond. In March the peasant follows the plough behind a yoke of oxen, while others tend the vines. In June, he is to be found scything the hay, while women rake and stack it. July is the month for sheep-shearing and reaping wheat with sickles, not scythes, and in August everyone strips off to swim in the river. The grape harvest falls in late September and the entire village turns out for it. In October the ground is tilled and prepared for seed, which the peasant flings out from a canvas pouch slung about his shoulders. Broadly speaking, this was the village that had evolved in the northern half of France by the end of the sixteenth century. But what of the south and the south-west?

The South

Conditions in the south gave rise to villages with specific local characteristics; because of their limited building space, the poverty of the land, political instability and their sheer remoteness, these ancient villages have remained much the same for some five hundred years. More by luck than by design, many of them have not – yet – fallen foul of motorway builders or town-planners.

Balazuc, Gard

Through the curious wrought-iron gate shaped into a sunburst and a star you can see that no *tuile-canale* (Roman tile) exactly matches its neighbour. But the overall effect of washed pink is only achieved with this blend of grey, ivory and orange. Modern tiles called *tuiles-mécaniques* have been used on the house in the background and are all of uniform colour. They are cheap and easy to lay since they have a hook moulded on the underside which slots neatly over the roof lath, but they will take some twenty years to weather and soften in colour.

Perched villages

There had been villages dotted about the low hilly plains in the hinterland of the Mediterranean coast since well before the Saracen invasions of the eighth century. Such communities fled before the invading armies as they marched into France up well-trodden routes, taking refuge in the rocky and inhospitable hills. A generation or two later, the same families straggled back to the plains, tempted by the better soil, richer pasture and good supplies of water, only to be sent back again by the next wave of invasion. Seigneurial ties were much weaker in the south, where there was a greater distribution of 'allodial' land, which a man could call his own, so the fierce attachment of a peasant to his plot was already deep-rooted. It was devastating to leave their land, but in the wake of Saxon and Lombard invasions the villagers gradually became herdsmen, and their mountain refuges became permanent homes.

The first homes were probably caves, hacked out and enlarged to create space for livestock and humans. Later most of the caves became stables and the family moved above ground, but not so long ago it was still quite common to live with the animals during the winter months in order to keep warm. A deep, wide runnel separated the two halves of the chamber and carried out waste, and sweet-smelling herbs were burnt to combat the smells. As the houses grew upwards the upper storeys leaned out over the street and met their opposite number, creating a little covered bridge called a *pontis* which cleverly buttressed the two houses. The steep streets, sometimes entirely vaulted in this way, were stepped, with a drainage channel running down the middle. At first the streets were hacked out of the bedrock, but when winter storms regularly washed away the top rubble, it became clear that the steepest would have to be paved, sometimes with smooth stones from the river bed. Stout fortifications of local stone surrounded the village, the blocks being laboriously quarried by hand and hauled up or down the precipitous mountain using primitive blocks and tackle, or loaded onto carts drawn by donkeys with a team of men pushing from behind. The outer ring of houses, and sometimes the church, were built into the ramparts, while the château always stood at the highest point, for together with the church it was the main look-out point and the last place of refuge should the ramparts be breached.

Scarcity of water and of cultivable land were the most intractable problems. Where there was space, cisterns were built to catch rainwater for common use, and one villager was appointed to supervise the distribution of the collected water, which was a precious reserve commodity to supplement or replace spring water during times of drought. Frequently the spring or stream

22

was some distance from the village, and such villages were particularly vulnerable to siege, for it was often a simple matter to block their water supply. In Cordes the villagers dug an immensely deep well – 110 metres – to prevent just this. In the distribution of land kitchen gardens occupied the flattest plots: they are still to be seen, strung down the hillside in terraces, planted with an impressive array of vegetables. In the Middle Ages, however, they would not have contained the tomatoes, peppers, pumpkins and marrows grown there today, for these were all imported from outside the kingdom, and did not become established in remote areas until well into the seventeenth century.

While one of the women tended the kitchen garden, one of the men took the goats or sheep to pasture in a field where he had built himself a stone shelter, called a *borie* in Provence. While the animals grazed he would set snares for rabbits or fish for trout, hoping to escape the eye of the gamekeeper, since poaching was an offence against the seigneur. But there were many mouths to feed at home, and some of the hard-won produce had to be sold to pay taxes. The best vegetables, eggs, chickens and fruit were all sent to market.

In his book *Montaillou*, Emmanuel Le Roy Ladurie describes the highly structured form of these close-knit communities, and the narrow line dividing stability from anarchy when large extended families lived beneath one roof, and permanently under the scrutiny of their neighbours. Internally there were family feuds, vendettas and promiscuity, but to the outside world the village presented a hostile and united front. Many people claim that little has changed since then, and the novels of the twentieth-century writers Jean Giono and Marcel Pagnol, especially Pagnol's *Jean de Florette* and *Manon des Sources*, describe a people that seem at root to have altered very little in six hundred years.

Bastides

Bastide derives from the Provençal *bastida* and from the French *bâtir*, to build. It was after the crusade against the Albigensian Cathars that Count Raymond VII of Toulouse built the precursors of the *bastides* in around 1240 to protect his people. Cordes was one of some forty that he founded, and the system proved to be economically sound: the Count increased his annual revenues from his territories fivefold in as many years. But *bastides* made military sense too, and by the mid-fourteenth century four or five hundred had been built. Almost all *bastides*

date from this time, and most of them grew from nothing into a garrison town within the space of five to ten years. Whereas most villages can trace their beginnings to before the year 1000 and many to pre-Roman times, *bastides* were built in a hurry when the first hostilities of the hundred years war between the French and the English broke out in Gascony and Guyenne. No sooner had the English forces begun one, than the French countered with another; in fact no one with land and a workforce to protect could afford not to follow suit. One of the most perfect in form and in preservation is Monpazier in the Dordogne.

For villagers, the opportunity of helping to build and then to populate a *bastide* really was a chance in a lifetime for it meant that they could make the leap from serfdom to freedom within a very short time. If a man undertook to lend his skills he would be granted his freedom, a house and a plot of land – the generosity of the offer being an indication of the drastic shortage of manpower at this time. This was the cause of a good deal of competition between the founders of the *bastides*; public criers were sent out to advertise the benefits a particular lord or baron could offer. *Bastides* were named after famous cities such as 'Pavie' or 'Bologne', or with reference to their supposed charms or advantages, such as 'Plaisance', 'Beaumont' or 'Villefranche'. When a nucleus of craftsmen and labourers had been acquired the *bastide* went up according to a careful plan designed to help it to withstand siege for much longer than older, haphazardly built and fortified towns. As a rule, at the centre of the town stood the market place, the covered *halles* with tiled roof and stone or wooden pillars, surrounded by houses arcaded at street level. The church and last sanctuary, well fortified, stood nearby. Around the market place the streets of the town lay in a rectangular grid pattern, with each 'block' holding no more than a dozen or so dwellings and sometimes considerably fewer. These 'islands' were in turn divided by alleys designed in principle to serve as fire-breaks, but which possibly doubled as drains and latrines. The entire rectangular settlement was surrounded by one or two sets of ramparts with gateways and watchtowers.

France's small villages, however remote, all in some way reflect the changes the country has faced in its tumultuous history. Villagers have coped with invasions, internal struggles, famine and plague, and it is to these, no doubt, that they owe their instinct for self-preservation and their ability to adapt and survive. So what, if anything, is left of traditional village life today? Perhaps the answer to that question lies in the landscape of France itself. The rivers, valleys and high plateaux have determined the outward character of the villages and the way of life necessary to

Loubressac, Lot

It is from the tiny, exquisite village of Loubressac that one of the best views in France can be seen. Loubressac stands watchfully at the highest point of a precipitous ridge with spectacular views over the River Dordogne as it winds beneath the massive blood-red walls of the château of Castelnau, past companies of poplars and alongside tight ranks of maize.

survive; and often the harder the struggle, the stronger has been the attachment to the land and the will to continue living there.

Clearly the villages least affected by the twentieth century are those which are most isolated, and which preserve a landscape of fields, tracks and isolated buildings that would have been roughly familiar to people five hundred years ago. The labourer repairing the stone walls is, in many respects, no different from his counterpart of 1480. If they are newly quarried, the stones will have been cut out of the same rock face, and if they are old they will already have done time as part of an earlier wall, for precious materials have always been re-used. He may be a *cantonnier*, hired by the commune to keep roads and walls in good repair, but he may just as easily be doing someone a favour, for the exchange of goods and services is still an integral part of village life. Lucienne, taking her goats to browse on Gabriel's land, will return the kindness with a weekly supply of small round goat cheeses, done according to his taste; Marc is ploughing Aline's field in return for a load of hay later in the year, and in the autumn they will all meet at Lucienne's house, to help her turn the freshly slaughtered pig into pâtés, sausages and salted hams. No matter how large or small the gesture, this interdependence is part of the fabric of village life. Old habits die hard, too: popular beliefs about the influence of the moon on agriculture still hold fast all over France. Children are taught never to cut wood when the moon is new, and always to sow maize and oats as it wanes, but potatoes as it waxes. Cabbages, too, should be planted out on the waning moon, to encourage the roots to take hold.

In the south, where the notorious depopulation of rural areas has continued steadily since the war, you wonder how much longer these traditions will last. But if change is taking place, it is not necessarily unwelcome. The deserted village houses have been bought by a new breed of villager for holidays or retirement. It is true that the village's intrinsic ties with the land are disappearing, but the new, part-time inhabitants have created a demand for skilled craftsmen – tilers, carpenters, stone-masons and joiners able to work *à l'ancienne* so that the architectural character of the village is not lost. So whether the houses are thatched and half-timbered with loam or flint-and-pebble infills, or of warm limestone with stone roofs, or of herringbone patterned bricks with slate roofs, or of grey volcanic rock with rust-coloured tiles, their ancient harmony with their natural surroundings is still very much alive.

The villages in this book are an unashamedly personal selection from hundreds across the breadth of the land that could equally claim a place among these pages.

Each of the thirty-three thousand communes (the smallest administrative unit) in France embraces a number of villages, some thriving and expanding into new suburbs, some completely deserted and some which are still lively communities without apparently having changed their physical character.

National and private conservation organizations have been established all over France and are responsible for protecting many villages from indiscriminate development. The modern *maison coquette* of the estate agents' blurbs, where you can almost see the breeze-blocks under the *style-du-pays* façade, do not belong in this book. The villages photographed here were shaped long ago, some in response to the landscape, like those tucked among vines in the bountiful hills of Burgundy and Alsace, and some inspite of it, as in the south and south-west, where the infertile mountains and inhospitable *causses* or limestone plateaux gave the security of remoteness and inaccessibility. Many of those that stand on the ancient pilgrim routes across France have long-since become lost backwaters but some of them have fortunately been saved when on the verge of extinction. Discovering these is a proud and exciting moment for every traveller, and it is thanks to the much-maligned tourist and his enjoyment of discovery that they are still there for us to find and delight in.

Alba, Ardèche

Alba was once a well-equipped Gallo-Roman town with a forum, baths, theatre and aqueduct, but it was destroyed by barbarians in the fourth century, and a new village developed over the ruins of the old. The squat sixteenth-century château and church barely emerge from the shallow roofs of Roman tiles that distinguish all the villages and towns as you travel south from here down the Rhône valley. The long trail of industrial development along the banks of the Rhône, although only ten kilometres away, is well hidden beyond the hills. Almond trees in blossom are a reminder that the nearest big town is Montélimar, the centre of the nougat-making industry. In the sixteenth century Olivier de Serres, known as the father of French agriculture, not only encouraged the planting of mulberry trees so that France could produce its own silk, but also imported almond trees from Asia and planted them on his experimental farm at Pradel a few miles away.

Ansouis, Vaucluse

From wherever you approach it, the village of Ansouis appears invitingly on the horizon. It is one of several villages in the wide Durance valley framed to the north by the long foaming crest of Mt Lubéron, but Ansouis is distinguished from the rest by the pretty Renaissance façade of its château. Built as a medieval fortress, it was enlarged in the seventeenth century when the remarkable hanging gardens planted with cypresses, pines and box were begun, and it has always been in the possession of the family of the Counts of Sabran. The sturdy bell-tower is topped by a disarmingly makeshift wrought-iron campanile, a common feature in Provence where they can be seen on town halls and some private houses. Italian ironsmiths brought the tradition to France, where the work has always been carried out by local artisans.

Ansouis, Vaucluse

Quarries in the hills behind Ansouis have supplied stonecutters with the material of their trade for centuries. The limestone is white, porous, easy to quarry and soft to cut, enabling them to produce work such as this delicately curved and perfectly graded flight of steps. Since wood is scarce in these parts it has been easier and cheaper to use stone wherever possible. As a result, even the most humble building can look quite grand.

Aurel, Vaucluse

At roughly the same time every year, the tail end of July and early August, lavender is picked in Provence and the unwanted stalks burned. Near Aurel, the fragrant, intoxicating smoke drifts through the hills and hangs in the narrow village streets. Even as you whirl down the motorway you cannot fail to get a whiff of it. Lavender is commercially grown in great quantities in Provence and the best strain comes from the high hills surrounding Aurel. When the flowers have been dried they are either put into lavender bags and sent to cities where they are sold in the street, or they are distilled into oil and essence which are used in perfume making in Grasse and elsewhere. The best places to buy lavender are the herb markets to be found in any medium-sized Provençal town, where it is sold alongside huge bunches of basil, marjoram, thyme, sage and countless ingredients for making tisane.

Autoire, Lot

Autoire is in the old province of Quercy, which takes its name from the many oak trees that grow in the area, *quercus* being the Latin for oak. The village was once largely inhabited by wealthy vineyard owners which is why many of the village houses resemble miniature châteaux. In about 1875, phylloxera destroyed most of France's vines and in the small-scale vineyards the well-off chatelain became, virtually overnight, the struggling farmer. The owner of the Château de Limargue, which stands close to the church and river, was assured of a livelihood as he also ran the village mill. Other villagers had to turn to sheep rearing and market gardening for a living. Ironically, the phylloxera insect came to France from America, and it was with disease-resistant American stocks that the vineyards were replanted.

As you walk into Autoire you become aware of the sheer joy that filled the Quercynois builder as he put stone on stone, tile on tile. Not for him the carefully planned street; he preferred a seductive disorder of turrets, barns, gable windows and *gentilhommières* that exactly suit this landscape.

Autoire, Lot

Behind every *gentilhommière*, or manor house, in Autoire another stands hidden. They provide constant surprise with their individually carved gable windows, towers, steep sweeping roofs and stone staircases leading to stone verandahs. All this apparent disarray is shaped into order with baked brown tiles, rough-cut blocks of limestone and mortar the colour of onion skins.

The land around Autoire is given over to smallholdings, and most houses were built with their own dovecote, either attached or free-standing. Pigeon droppings provided a precious and continuous supply of manure for the fields, and on a farmer's death the droppings were carefully divided among the inheritors.

In late summer, the walnut trees begin to bend as the nuts swell, and Reine Claude plums appear in quantities in shops and markets alongside fresh garlic, melons and peaches. In the autumn the woods promise rich pickings of mushrooms — *chanterelles*, *cèpes* and *trompettes de la mort*, a black trumpet-shaped fungus which is not poisonous but looks and sounds it.

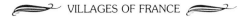
Autoire, Lot

The village houses in Autoire are built of creamy limestone from the Segonzac quarries, and their floors are made from the oaks that clothe the sides of the valley.

After the nineteenth-century phylloxera epidemic many of Autoire's smallholders replanted the land with *chênes truffiers*, the oak under whose root system the truffle most readily grows, and after ten years of careful preparation the fragrant black fungus appeared in quantities. But the First World War took the men away from the land and the old skills were not passed on.

Auvillar, Tarn-et-Garonne

In 1152 the broad, rich, agricultural area south and east of Bordeaux was brought into English hands with the marriage of Eleanor of Aquitaine with Henry Plantagenet and consequently became the object of a tug of war between Capetians and Plantegenets. The treaty of Paris in 1258 was intended to resolve the differences between the two dynasties and establish a fairer, if delicately balanced, distribution of territory between them; but by this time and because of the vagueness of the territorial borders, the two adversaries had begun to establish towns to defend themselves. These towns were purpose-built, like twentieth-century new towns, and took about five years to complete. They are called *bastides*, and Auvillar is a fine example.

Auvillar,
Tarn-et-Garonne

Auvillar, or Altum Villare, stands some way above the wide and airy Garonne valley. Until the nineteenth century it had its own thriving commercial port down by the river. Its market square, the heart of the village, is triangular with a circular market hall in the middle. The brick-built houses round the square form arcades, often found in *bastides*, providing shelter from rain and sun for pedestrians and for stall-holders selling farm produce such as cereals, garlic, melons, ducks and geese. It was not a simple task to build and then populate a *bastide*, and only the best incentives persuaded people to move in: owning your own home and farmland meant you were a free man, and the promise of such freedom was the finest incentive of all. Some *bastides* took their names from prestigious cities such as Florence (Fleurance) and Cordoba (Cordes), while others were given inviting names like Plaisance and Beaumont.

Balazuc, Gard

The River Ardèche flows beneath the walls of Balazuc, its water a limpid green over a bed of white gravel and sand. The village, once fortified, was also protected by the natural defences of the vertical valley sides. The first long-term settlers to take charge of this part of the valley were the Saracens in the eighth century. Today, local people who have crimped hair and an unusually dark skin are thought to be of Saracen descent.

Balazuc, Gard

Making the barest of livings was hard in Balazuc: the soil lies in pockets in the limestone called dolines and supports a few vines and the odd patch of rye. Silk-worm breeding provided a certain security until the infectious disease *pébrine* ensured only the fittest and wealthiest farms survived. The slow but implacable drift of rural people to the cities began in earnest at the turn of the century, and one by one the tall old foursquare houses became much prized summer homes.

The village house in Balazuc was built on the principle of keeping the most valuable possessions very near to you, in this case livestock: sheep, goats, a pig and some racks of silk-worms. Silk-worm farming, well established in southern France even before the growth of Lyon gave it a new industrial meaning, was often responsible for the shape of the houses; the eggs needed a constant warm temperature for incubation, and once hatched the worms had to be kept on stacked racks in rooms tall enough to accommodate them. The incubation rooms usually had four chimneys, one in each corner, to keep an ambient temperature; a small-scale farmer with less room to spare might have asked his wife to keep a clutch of eggs warm in her bodice. The industry declined in the early 1920s when *pébrine* appeared, and the villagers of Balazuc were forced to tighten their belts and scrape a living from the soil.

Bargemon, Var

The buildings in Bargemon are constructed from roughly quarried chunks of calcareous stone held together with a mortar of sand and lime. By late afternoon, the houses are warm with the heat of the sun, and the scent of orange blossom and mimosa is at its most intense. Bargemon, sheltered from the wilder weather of Provence because it sits just under the Provençal plateau, has a mild and pleasant climate. For centuries it has been an assembly point for all local produce, and specialized until the nineteenth century in annual fairs for trading in wool and leather. Ruins of fortifications belonging to a twelfth-century castle and a fine gateway in the Place de la Mairie remind you that this was once a well-defended town. The little chapel of Notre-Dame de Montaigu has a spire which pinpoints the spot to which pilgrims first came in the seventeenth century to pay homage to an olive-wood statue of the Virgin which had been brought from Belgium by a local monk.

Baume-les-Messieurs, Jura

The modest but pretty River Seille rises at Baume-les-Messieurs and then winds its way through a fortress-like valley until it reaches the southward-flowing Saône. The village originated in the sixth century when a group of monks, inspired by the setting, its plentiful supply of pure water and its dramatically unpredictable climate, determined to found a community. Four hundred years later the still-thriving community moved from its humble village accommodation into the splendid monastery founded by Bienheureux Bernonen, a monk of the Cluny order. Baume derives from *balma* meaning cavern, while Messieurs was the term given to monks of noble birth.

Baume-les-Messieurs, Jura

As the monastery of Baume-les-Messieurs grew, so did the village surrounding it. The need for security and refuge was just as important in the Middle Ages as having a nearby supply of clean water. The villagers made a living from the soil, mainly from growing vines and making wine. The vines covered the lower slopes of the hills and grew right up to the walls of the houses and to the edge of the river.

Most wine-growers, or *vignerons*, in Baume-les-Messieurs kept a few head of cattle stabled in the lower half of their houses for milk and meat. The family lived above the stable in rooms reached by an exterior staircase. Also at street level was the *cave* or cellar. Behind its solid oak doors stood the winepress and the pressing stones.

Les Baux, Bouches-du-Rhône

Les Baux, because of its spectacular position on a high spur of the Alpilles, is one of the most frequently visited villages in all of Provence. But it is almost entirely in ruins and only a few inhabitants remain. It is in the evening when the visitors have left that the real spirit of Les Baux returns: then the wild and freedom-loving *seigneurs des Baux*, who for centuries held out defiantly against would-be combatants, seem to re-inhabit these gaunt, old ruins and gaze on the war-torn plain below.

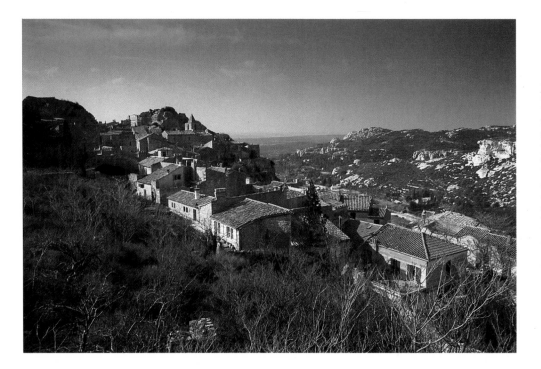

In the fourteenth century under the notorious Raymond de Turenne the village became a bandit centre. Captives were held in the dungeon on the highest point of the rock and, if their supporters were unable or unwilling to raise the ransom asked, they were allowed to take a last look at the dramatic view spread out below and then were thrown over the edge of the cliff. Les Baux was famous for its obstinate refusal to bow to other lords, but equally for being one of the most renowned courts of love in the Midi, where troubadours composed formal verses dedicated to love. The Baux family claimed to be descended from Balthazar, one of the Magi, and included a star of Bethlehem in their arms. The family line died out late in the fourteenth century and the village's glittering life came to an end.

The village revived in the early nineteenth century when a new mineral, bauxite, named after the village, was discovered in 1822.

Beynac, Dordogne

If you travel the Dordogne valley towards the west you come to the village of Beynac, pressed against the rock face between river and plateau and dominated by its thirteenth-century château. This formidable stronghold was held in 1189 by the dreaded Mercadier, whose men terrorized the surrounding countryside in the name of Richard the Lionheart. In 1214, Simon de Montfort dismantled the château as part of his campaign against the Albigensian, or Cathar, heretics. When that period of persecution and inquisition was over, the Baron of Beynac rebuilt his domain which quickly became a French military stronghold in the Hundred Years War.

Across the river from Beynac and clearly visible from the village, stand the ruins of the château of Castelnaud, where Simon de Montfort lived while he was hounding the Cathars in about 1215. The Hundred Years War brought the English to Castelnaud, and with Beynac loyal to the king of France the two strongholds stared one another out implacably, like waiting cats, occasionally making bloody sorties to raid each other's territory. Fields of maize and tobacco now cover the old skirmishing grounds.

Beynac, Dordogne

The château of Beynac remained in the hands of the same family of barons for more than five hundred years until the 1950s. Since then it has been in the process of meticulous restoration under the auspices of the French Government. The materials, workmanship and structural repairs are subject to the approval of the state-run organization Bâtiments de France, which has an office in each *département*. The principal architect for each office is responsible for checking the suitability of all materials used in restoration work, and plans for restoring any building near a *site classé*, such as these near the château of Beynac, must always be referred to the architect for approval.

Blesle, Haute-Loire

Somewhere beneath the streets of Blesle are the foundations of the Roman villa of Blaseus. The villa stood at the confluence of four rivers: the Sianne, Voireuse, Bellan and Alagnon. In the ninth century a group of Benedictine nuns, all of noble birth, founded an abbey near the site of the villa. The abbess was the town's seigneur, and she and her nuns led a pleasant life, each with her own house overlooking the main quadrangle of the abbey. The village of Blesle grew up close to the abbey walls, the villagers giving farm produce in return for protection from the agressive Catholic Mercoeur barons who were steadily encroaching on their freedom and security. The abbey church of St Pierre, with its 800-year-old doors, was their parish church and their refuge.

Blesle, Haute-Loire

The dark, grim basalt of most of Blesle's houses has been partly covered in a lighter roughcast of lime. Great cliffs of the igneous rock have been formed where the Sianne and Alagnon rivers have cut gorges from east to west, and Blesle lies in a quiet, heavily wooded valley under a sombre rocky escarpment. The rivers dissect the high granite plateau called the Cézallier where cattle are taken to graze in the summer months. At one time the cowherds would leave their homes and spend five months in a small stone thatched hut called a *buron*, but since the Cézallier was enclosed most of the huts are now redundant.

Bonnieux, Vaucluse

The Roman tiles, or *tuiles-canales,* that give the roofs in Bonnieux their rich texture and colour are shaped out of clay on a wooden mould. In the past, the potter moulded each tile over his thigh. They are ideally suited to the climate of Provence, but sometimes can be seen as far north as the Loire and Lorraine. A covering of tiles, hollow-side up, is laid on the roof over a lattice of wood, and a second layer is made by placing the tiles hollow-side down over the edges of the tiles below. These tiles have helped determine the familiar shallow planes of a Provençal village skyline; the roofs, sometimes weighted with stones, present the least resistance to the wind and their shallowness discourages the tiles from slipping.

Bonnieux, Vaucluse

The lower northern slopes of Mt Lubéron send out long, finger-like promontories towards Apt and the valley of the River Coulon. On one of these spurs stands Bonnieux, spread out now beyond the confining thirteenth-century walls but none the less losing nothing of its charm. A series of rough stone staircases and terraces wind their way to a belvedere at the top of the town and to a captivating little twelfth-century church surrounded by sentinel-like cypresses.

Many houses in villages all over France are like pictures within pictures. This elegant flight of steps in Bonnieux leads through an imposing doorway only to reveal an almost identical arrangement of stairways and entrances in the courtyard, and yet another peaceful courtyard beyond the first.

Bonnieux, Vaucluse

Bonnieux is one of four villages each on its own hilly peninsula that watch each other across the vineyards and hazy fields of lavender in the Coulon valley. The others are Ménerbes, Oppède-le-Vieux and Lacoste, the last being the eighteenth-century home of the irrepressible Marquis de Sade. Lacoste had been, some three centuries before, the neighbour that Bonnieux loved to hate. The villagers were in the habit of kidnapping the Catholic provost and consuls of Bonnieux and demanding heavy ransoms for their return. In his day de Sade, inspite of his record, was known as *le divin marquis* though according to his letters the ladies of neighbouring towns and villages found him wonderfully fearsome and thought he was a werewolf.

Brantes, Vaucluse

Brantes is the village nearest the foot of Mt Ventoux, the most western outpost of the southern Alps before the Rhône valley, and the most dominating geological presence in the landscape. It is 2,000 metres high and, true to its name, is almost always windswept. The mistral, that depressing wind which blows down the Rhône valley, clips the side of the mountain and has turned the upper half into a stony desert, while the lower half, re-afforested in the nineteenth century, is covered in a rich variety of trees and plants.

Cabrerets, Lot

It is only in winter that the compact village of Cabrerets can be seen as a whole, when the poplars lining the banks of the River Célé are bare of leaves. The château of Gontaut-Biron, standing shoulder high to the church, is defended at its back by steep scrub-covered hills with rocky outcrops of grey limestone protruding like bones from the land. In 1922, two fourteen-year-old schoolboys were walking over this rocky plateau, exploring its faults and cracks, when their dog disappeared under a bush. It concealed a hole in the roof of a cave system and the boys had discovered the Pech-Merle cave and its 20,000-year-old paintings. It was not until 1949 that the real entrance to the cave was found.

Callas, Var

The multistorey houses at Callas seem possessively to guard the village church. Indeed, one of them shares a wall with the church and acts as a buttress. It is not an uncommon sight to find houses used as supports in this way. Romanesque churches were built tall and spacious, but the weight of the barrel-vaulted roofs meant windows had to be small and the walls supported to take the strain, making the already austere nave rather sombre too. Callas is one of a group of tiny medieval villages in this pretty wooded part of the Var valley, and for years was only accessible by foot. Today, in the worst winter weather, the roads can be impassable for weeks on end.

Cardaillac, Lot

The oldest part of Cardaillac, north-west of Figeac, is its fort. Built in the twelfth century on a triangular site it has views across to the wooded slopes of the Drauzou valley. Cardaillac's proudest possessions are the two towers of the fort that are still standing. The square Sagnes tower, which can be visited, has two vaulted rooms stacked above each other and is topped by a flat terrace. The other is known as the Baron's tower, and its rakishly tilted roof contains a dovecote where doves were kept not for message carrying but for their fertile droppings which were used as manure.

The towers of Cardaillac's fort rise out of the village looking oddly grandiose today, though in the twelfth century the fort was the home of the local seigneur. The roof to a tower was either conical, flat or pitched. If it collapsed it was sometimes re-roofed, like the Baron's tower on the right. This work was evidently done in a hurry, since there was not time to level off the tower walls.

Carennac, Lot

The heart of Carennac and the reason for its existence is its priory, which was founded in the tenth century, fortified, much damaged during the Revolution and finally disbanded in 1788 when it was sold. The village that clings to the priory church lines the waterside under a cool canopy of chestnut and poplar trees, and wriggles backwards away from the river in a maze of narrow, tranquil streets.

It is said that this tower, known as Télémaque's tower, is where Fénelon wrote his masterpiece *Les Aventures de Télémaque* in 1699. Fénelon was a theology student at Cahors while his uncle was prior of Carennac in the late seventeenth century. When his uncle died, Fénelon succeeded him as prior and became much loved and greatly revered. In those days the Dordogne was a busy river route carrying raftloads of cargo as well as passengers down to Bordeaux, and Fénelon used to arrive at Carennac by boat. One can conjure up an intriguing sound picture of Carennac as a noisy, bustling and competitive waterside town, quite different to its present museum-like hush.

Carennac, Lot

The glory of Carennac is the doorway to its twelfth-century church, where a sculpture of Christ in Majesty raises his hand in blessing on the four evangelists and, indeed, on all laymen as they approach this door. What you see is a bearded Christ whose robe falls in straight and narrow folds close to his body, the figure radiating stillness filled with vigour. The sculpture is in a style known as the Toulouse school, other examples of which can be seen at Beaulieu, Moissac and Collonges. Some people believe that these bold and original early craftsmen were summoned to work on the great Gothic tympana of Chartres and Rheims cathedrals.

Chamelet, Rhône

If you have the good fortune to see Chamelet for the first time in the setting sun, you will understand why this part of the Beaujolais is called the *pays des pierres dorées* – land of golden stones – for the limestone walls of the houses, drab on a grey day, take up a warm brilliance at sunset. Slotted into each other with tailored perfection, the stones bear witness to the fine craftsmanship handed down from father to son in the village. Chamelet overlooks the valley of the Azergues, where the landscape, free from the pressures of wine production further north, is tranquil. Orchards, vineyards and vegetable gardens all have their place around the village, and sheep graze near the ruins of the old feudal fortifications. As you walk along the only street, you pass beneath a series of small market halls with tiled roofs resting on oak pillars, built by an imaginative local *bourgeois* in the sixteenth century.

Chas, Puy-de-Dôme

Chas is an intricate tangle of medieval streets surrounding a sturdy little sixteenth-century church. The brick-built houses are covered in a soft-apricot-coloured rendering while the corners, lintels and village fountains are of grey lava from the Puy-de-Dôme volcanoes.

Although only twenty-five kilometres from Clermont-Ferrand, capital of Auvergne, Chas's identity lies with the surrounding wonderfully fertile farmland and with the north-flowing River Allier. Fields of wheat, beetroot, maize and tobacco cover these low plains, known as the Limagne, which extend from the Dôme mountains in the west to the granite massifs of the Livradois and Forez in the east. Probably the oldest crop grown here is garlic, introduced by wealthy monasteries in the Middle Ages.

Collonges-la-Rouge, Corrèze

Chunks of raw red sandstone are the building blocks of Collonges. There is no other village quite this extraordinary colour in all France. The dominant feature of Collonges is a Romanesque church with bell-tower and big sturdy keep, its battlemented watchtower once in permanent use. Butting up against the church are the other essential parts of a village, the market square and hall; in Collonges a bread oven is incorporated into this ensemble, and the long-handled paddle used to extract the baked loaves still hangs there. Some of the villagers remember taking bread and pastries to the communal oven on baking day. The last items in, as the oven cooled, were meringues. Meat dishes were always cooked in a pot over an open fire.

The centre of Collonges is small and the houses quite modest, but as you walk down a series of tranquil narrow lanes that lead you into the surrounding countryside there are a number of small and exquisite châteaux.

Collonges-la-Rouge, Corrèze

Lord of Collonges in the sixteenth century was Gédéon de Vassignac. His house (pictured here) is like a fairy-tale castle, with little turrets and mullioned windows. Vassignac was a staunch Protestant, like all the people of the Viscounty of Turenne which covered a large area of Corrèze. Many of the officers of the Viscounty owned summer residences in Collonges, and you can tell that these manor houses were designed principally for pleasure: cool flagged courtyards lead you from one wing to another, and each house is set in charming landscaped gardens looking towards a carefully chosen stretch of countryside, with banks and terraces shaded by walnut trees and chestnuts leading away from the main house.

The master craftsman in charge of the finest stonecutting was entitled to leave his mark on his work. The keystone of this Collonges doorway is carved with a star, while others simply carry sets of initials. Each stone was hand-cut, some roughly for domestic purposes such as barns, market places and village houses, and others carefully shaped for a church or manor house. Inevitably, architecture in Collonges is a mixture of styles from the three surrounding areas: Périgord, Limousin and Quercy.

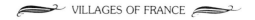

Collonges-la-Rouge, Corrèze

The little roofed galleries called *bolets* used for drying chestnuts, maize and tobacco, are typical of the Périgord region; the flat grey tiles, sometimes synonymous with wealth, are more common around Limoges, and the *pigeonnier* is pure Quercy. All three areas borrow from each other's styles, and the same characteristics can be found much further afield.

Conques, Aveyron

The glint of sunlight on grey schist roofs emerging from the wooded slopes of the Ouche valley informed the medieval pilgrim that he was nearing Conques. Today, if you approach the village from the east following the valley the first sighting would not be dissimilar to his. Lying on the old pilgrims' way to Santiago de Compostela, Conques has always been a staging post for weary travellers. Its monastery, founded in the eighth century, was one of the most powerful in France and itself became a place for pilgrimage.

Conques, Aveyron

In the ninth century the abbey of Conques acquired the relics of Sainte Foy, a young Christian girl who had been martyred in Agen two centuries earlier: the curious reliquary containing her skull is still in the present church. With the advent of this asset the once quiet village assumed a position of some prominence on the Catholic map. Wealth poured in from visiting nobles, and the village thrived on the new business they and their retinues brought in. By the mid-twelfth century a new abbey church had been built on a natural terrace overlooking the gorge. The church marks the passage from Romanesque to Gothic architecture. The red sandstone and yellow limestone from the local quarries of Nauviale and Lunel marry nicely with the tawny village houses. Within its wide walls is one of France's richest stores of gold, silver and religious statuary, and the tympanum above the west door depicting the Last Judgement is an arresting example of Romanesque Auvergne art.

The sparkling grey tiles that characterize nearly every roof in the village are a hallmark of the Rouergue regional building style: hand cut, thick and rough, they are outstanding insulators against frost and summer sun. A Rouergue tiler will use large squarish tiles for the edges and angles of a roof, gradually picking smaller ones, rounded like scales, as he approaches the middle. Properly tiled, a roof like this is almost indestructible and will keep a house and its dwellers safe and dry for generations.

Cordes, Tarn

'Cordes-sur-ciel', as it is called, stands on an isolated spur above the valley of the Cérou. Cordes is a *bastide*, purpose-built by Raymond VII, Count of Toulouse, to protect his subjects against the Crusaders. In the early thirteenth century widespread anti-clerical feeling in France gave rise to heretical movements, one of which, the Cathar or Albigensian heresy, permeated the whole of southern French society and became a real threat to political stability. It was when Simon de Montfort, at the Pope's behest, began his campaign against the Albigensians that Count Raymond built Cordes, naming it after the Spanish town of Córdoba in Andalucía. Great blocks of local limestone formed three massive sets of ramparts within which the village quickly sprang up: a well was sunk over a hundred metres deep, and grain was stored in excavations in the hillside itself.

The Huguenot uprisings of the sixteenth and seventeenth centuries and a bout of plague that followed put an end to Cordes's well-earned tranquil existence, and the village's isolation was nearly its undoing. Some of the nobler houses were restored in the nineteenth century – one of them, the Maison du Grand Fauconnier, by the great French writer and architect Viollet-le-Duc, who also restored Notre-Dame in Paris and the ancient city of Carcassonne. (The nineteenth-century novelist Prosper Merimée gave the house its name after the falcon heads emerging from the façade.) It was not until the 1940s that Cordes found a new role as host to artisans and artists in search of just such a remote and romantic workplace. The founder of the new community was the French painter Yves Brayer. With impetus from him the more modest, half-timbered fourteenth-century houses were restored.

Coursegoules, Alpes-Maritimes

Though only a crow's flight from the twentieth-century hum of the Côte d'Azur, Coursegoules feels remote and separate in the arid country above and to the west of the River Var. It is tucked into the foot of Mt Cheiron and overlooks the source waters of the River Cagne. The multistorey houses all vie for the fairest view across the valley, each stretching above the other; but tallest of all is the church which dominates the village from the back. Inside the church there is an altarpiece by Louis Bréa of John the Baptist flanked by St Petronella and St Gothard. Bréa and other sixteenth-century painters worked largely for penitent brotherhoods, and that is why their works can be found in many scattered and isolated churches and chapels.

La Couvertoirade, Aveyron

The walls, towers, castle and church of La Couvertoirade still stand preserved, if not perfectly at least enough for us to imagine the chink of mail as the white-robed Templars and the Hospitallers of St John paced the ramparts and stood guard at the gates. When part of the Larzac plateau was given to the Templars in the twelfth century they established a *commanderie* at Ste Eulalie and two dependencies, one at La Couvertoirade, the other at La Cavalerie. There is a paved dew pond, or *lavogne*, outside the walls which is still used today and would certainly have been in use in the days of the Templars. The ewes that drink at such ponds produce the milk which becomes one of the world's best blue cheeses: Roquefort.

La Couvertoirade, Aveyron

La Couvertoirade is one of the best-preserved Templar fortress villages in France. Situated on the highest part of the remote Larzac plateau, it is surrounded by an arid and bare landscape patterned with rough-stone walls and outcrops of grey limestone. From the twelfth to the fourteenth centuries the Knights Templars and then the Hospitallers occupied this village and others in south-west France. Many of the villages are overgrown ruins, sometimes identifiable by a distinguishing cross cut into the stone. But long after the orders of the warrior-monks had been disbanded, La Couvertoirade continued to be an important stopping place for pilgrims travelling to Santiago de Compostela along the lonely road between Millau and Lodève.

Helped with the heavy work by his neighbours, some of whom had special skills such as roofing or stonecutting, a villager would build his own house in a small remote village like La Couvertoirade. The layout of each of the village houses followed the same pattern: livestock was kept on the ground floor, and an outside stone staircase led to the first-floor living quarters which in winter would benefit from the warmth generated by the animals below. It was and still is customary in some homes to cook, eat, sleep and welcome neighbours in the same large first-floor room.

In general, the spirit of the community saw to it that no one was left wanting. There was a village bread oven, and a communal cistern fed by rainwater from the church roof. Outside the village wheat was grown in the rich, red, clayey soil that gathered in depressions in the limestone sometimes no more than ten or twenty yards wide.

Domme, Dordogne

Domme in the Périgord region of the Dordogne has seen violence, struggled to survive and changed masters in this once turbulent part of France, but it has never really succumbed to external influences or lost its true identity. The tip-tilted roofs, the delicate carving of stone lintels and gable fronts, the grace of the finished house, however humble, is reassuring proof that practicality and beauty can be achieved together.

From Domme, on top of its sheer rocky crag, you can look down onto a quintessential Périgord scene: the River Dordogne shoulders its way past crowding bone-coloured cliffs of limestone on one side, slim poplars and cultivated fields neat as a naïve painting on the other. Domme lies tranquilly under the sun on its splendid site, but its walls and ramparts reveal a history of siege, upheaval and heroic acts of daring. In 1586 the village was taken by the Huguenots, who were much given to military trickery. Thirty men and their leader entered the sleeping town via the precipitous rock face called the Barre and made such a racket that the inhabitants were thrown into disarray. In the mêlée that followed, the saboteurs opened the gates and let in the rest of the Huguenot soldiers. Their leader Geoffroi de Vivans took charge and burnt down all Catholic churches and meeting places.

Domme, Dordogne

Under Domme's streets lies a network of underground passages and caves that once contained evidence of prehistoric dwellings. During the Hundred Years War and the wars of religion, the people of Domme hid in the caves among the ancient stalactites and stalagmites while warring armies clashed outside the city walls. During the German occupation, Resistance workers used the caves as a refuge, but their hiding places were exposed by collaborators and they were shot.

Entrevaux, Alpes-de-Haute-Provence

Entrevaux sits at the knee of a bare outcrop of rock, its walls, roofs and ramparts faded to delicate creamy pinks by wind, rain and sun. A fortified way punctuated by defensive gateways zigzags downhill to the village from an eighteenth-century citadel. These impressive defences were designed and built by Sébastien, Marquis de Vauban, the great military engineer and architect of Louis XIV, and one of France's heroes. For forty years his engineering skill took him all over France, rubbing shoulders with rich and poor alike. His understanding of the privileges of the former and the problems of the latter led him to propose an entirely new fiscal system which, however, gained the support of neither the king nor the council, and Vauban died dejected soon afterwards.

Entrevaux, Alpes-de-Haute-Provence

Entrevaux has changed little since the eighteenth century when it was fortified to defend the border with the duchy of Savoy, the frontier being the River Var which loops round the town and ramparts just to the north. As you walk through one of the three main gates with its working portcullis you emerge into the twisting streets of the old village, cool and shady even at noon in summer. The seventeenth-century cathedral, seat of a bishop until the Revolution, is built into the outer ramparts; next to it is a tall crenellated bell-tower which was built by the Knights Templars in the eleventh century.

Estaing, Aveyron

The fifteenth- and sixteenth-century château at Estaing is today inhabited by a religious community, but the ascendance of the powerful Estaing family can be traced by observing how the roughly assembled early outer walls of the château yield gradually to the later and much more intricate stonework of the interior. Medieval houses, many of them now abandoned, are crammed together in the space between château and church. They all bear the same distinguishing marks that characterize this quiet little town: grey schist roofs tiled in fish-scale patterns, wide portals at street level to allow cattle inside, roofs designed to give the maximum grain and hay storage beneath and balconies under overhanging eaves used for drying maize, chestnuts and tobacco. The elegant terrace of houses by the river was built in the eighteenth century, and its uncluttered design reflects the simplicity of the medieval bridge that crosses the River Lot.

Estaing, Aveyron

Although Estaing is associated with the burial of St Fleuret's body some time before the seventh century, its fame derives from the Estaing family who gave it its name and especially Jean-Baptiste Estaing. Born in 1729, he served France as a naval officer abroad fighting the British. On his return the Revolution was at its height and he was welcomed as a hero and made an admiral. But his loyalty was to the king, and following the discovery of his plans to help the royal family escape he was tried and condemned to death. At the guillotine he said to his captors, 'When you have my head, send it to the English. They will pay you well for it'.

Gordes, Vaucluse

Gordes spills down the sides of the rocky Vaucluse plateau becoming an unpredictable maze of houses, caves, impossibly narrow streets, flights of steps and covered alleys; a place where it is hard to distinguish between the village and the rock from which it is built.

France's most famous collection of *bories*, vaulted dry-stone shepherds' huts, is a short way from the village. Built of large flat *lauze* (roofing stones) placed one on the other until a perfect vaulted roof has been formed, they have walls at least three feet thick, no windows and no chimney. It is said that during the great plague people fled from Gordes to the *bories* village to save themselves.

Gordes became an artists' colony created by Victor Vasarély in the 1960s. Today, many of the huts are being converted into second homes.

La Grave, Hautes-Alpes

La Traverse, one of La Grave's main streets, is part of the old coaching route from Briançon to Grenoble. The journey by coach must have been frightening, uncomfortable and breathtaking all at once. La Grave is set in an exceptionally lush valley surrounded by the pine forests, glaciers and snowy peaks that form part of a huge complex of ski-runs covering the southern Alps. One of the characters in Honoré de Balzac's book *le Médicin de Campagne*, is modelled on an inhabitant of La Grave (a *Gravarot*), who would undoubtedly have lived in one of the smart buildings near the church – proximity to God's house being a measure of social standing. The Romanesque style survives in the architecture of the seventeenth-century church.

Hunawihr, Haut-Rhin

Hunawihr is one of the villages on the *route du vin d'Alsace*. This is no new tourist trail but a way familiar since before the Middle Ages, though only officially designated as a *route* in 1951. The village fits snugly between the low-lying Alsace plain and the higher forests of the Vosges mountains, surrounded by its one and only crop for centuries: the grape. Alsace has produced wine since prehistoric times, but cultivation began in earnest only after the Roman Conquest, with the Rhine providing transport. The vineyards, owned by convents and monasteries, were so productive in the Middle Ages that a Franciscan monk from Thann wrote: 'This year (1431) the wine is so cheap and plentiful that since we are short of barrels we are using it to mix mortar'.

Most of the old village was built in the sixteenth century: if the houses seem modest, the real wealth of the Hunawihr *bourgeois* is displayed in the sumptuousness of the Gothic town hall (1517) and the beauty of the earlier fortified church.

Locronan, Finistère

The cobbled main square of Locronan is enclosed by terraces of granite Renaissance houses built to complement the fifteenth-century church and the adjoining chapel of le Pénity. Inside the chapel stands the massive tomb of Saint Ronan, from whom the village takes its name. He was an Irish monk who came to Brittany in the fifth century and lived near Locronan as a hermit, steadily converting the Bretons to Christianity. *Loc* means holy place in Breton, and every year the saint is remembered in well-attended religious processions to the accompaniment of drums and bugles.

The fifteenth century saw the beginning of a fast-growing sailcloth weaving industry in Brittany, and Locronan suddenly began to prosper, supplying sails to the ships of the king's navy. The next two centuries were Locronan's finest years, and Breton fleets regularly set out for South America and the Far East. As you approach the church and its square the houses begin to reflect the prosperity of their merchant owners; the wealthiest clearly lived on the prime spot, in the square itself. Some of the houses carry obvious status symbols such as stone-mullioned dormer windows and door lintels worked in granite decorated with Christian or pagan signs.

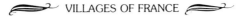

Loubressac, Lot

From its balcony position Loubressac was able to survey any military activity in the plain below, where the rivers Cère and Bave join the Dordogne. The village had four main entrances on its landward side, heavily fortified against intruders. Despite these defences it was largely destroyed in the Hundred Years War and not re-inhabited until the fifteenth century.

The road to Loubressac is lined with walnut trees and Reine Claude plums, which grow more abundantly here than anywhere else in France. The road leads into a sloping square with pools of deep shade under the trees, surrounded by old houses with brown tiled roofs and mellowed limestone walls.

Loubressac, Lot

From Loubressac's square you can pass through one of the remaining gates of the village and wander through narrow streets, past medieval houses with bending hollyhocks, clusters of geraniums in pots and cool trellises heavy with vines.

Lucéram, Alpes-Maritimes

The two ravines that flank Lucéram on either side form corridors down which sweep huge banks of cloud in winter. The picture in summer is quite different: the tall fifteenth-century church tower emerges white against the dark green mountainside, dominating the surrounding cluster of medieval houses, all of which are at least three storeys high. To enlarge the living area, some are joined at first floor level to form a bridge over the street called a *pontis*. The tower set into fortifications at the far end of Lucéram was deliberately built open on the village side to prevent enemies taking it and attacking the village. Inside the church are some of the most outstanding works by the now-famous Louis Bréa, a sixteenth-century painter from Nice recognized as one of Provence's great artists.

98

Marcilhac-sur-Célé, Lot

The River Célé running westward
from Figeac cuts its way through
the limestone plateau of the
Causse de Cajarc, creating a
deep incision from Figeac to
Cahors. On the narrow strip of
land along its banks are fields of
tobacco and maize, tobacco
drying grounds and plantations
of walnut trees. Marcilhac lies
peacefully under the eye of the
huge and brooding limestone
cliffs and alongside the River
Célé which flows quietly past the
village's working flour mill and
on towards Sauliac.

They are *boules* fanatics in
Marcilhac, and on Sundays after
Mass all the villagers turn out to
watch or play on the open grassy
space that slopes from the war
memorial on the main street to
the river's edge. Half hidden by
the old village houses are the
evocative ruins of an
eleventh-century Benedictine
abbey which is open to the sky
and, even in high summer, is
usually cool and deserted. The
abbot's house stood near the
river just beyond the war
memorial.

Méailles, Alpes-de-Haute-Provence

High up on the east bank of the River Vaire, the remote village of Méailles is tacked like rickrack along a jagged seam of limestone, formed some sixty million years ago as the earth's crust folded and the upper layer of Jurassic limestone was squeezed out and forced upwards. Weather erosion has formed the white ridges and outcrops that look as if the skeleton of the land is emerging from the earth. Linking the villages in the valley of the Vaire is the railway running from Digne to Nice. It is a spectacular feat of engineering since it runs through more kilometres of tunnel than open air. The lavender which grows wild in this rocky landscape was gathered and sold at local markets until its commercial possibilities were noticed, and the familiar cultivated giant tufts in their formal lines began to change the face of the land.

Ménerbes, Vaucluse

It is a sad fact that the countless little hill-top villages like Ménerbes which grew up in the early Middle Ages are now more museum pieces than living communities. When battles for supremacy raged on the fertile plains among Saxons, Saracens and Lombards, small medieval agricultural communities were forced to the relative safety of high ground where they scratched a living out of the poor soil. The communities abandoned the hill-top villages and moved back to the plains when peaceful stability returned. Ménerbes runs along the flank of a ridge extending outwards from Mt Lubéron, looking rather like a basking seal draped over a rock with at its head a castle, and stretched out behind a line of houses steadily decreasing in splendour with the poorest dwellings at the end. These houses are half built into the rock and were once troglodyte homes before being enlarged by new settlers. The little corner house in the picture shows how economy and imagination have made of a cave a most desirable cottage.

Monpazier, Dordogne

Edward I of England and Duke of Aquitaine founded Monpazier in 1284. It is one of the most beautiful of the *bastide* villages, due in part to the pleasing ordered logic of its design. The walled rectangular town has a grid pattern of streets which originally divided it into forty-two blocks, each an independently defensible island and thus protected somewhat from the risk of spreading fire. The square at the centre is surrounded by a spectacular vaulted way passing under the houses, designed to allow mounted horsemen, as well as pedestrians, access to the arcades. This is where the corn market was held and where today *cèpes*, the most delectable of fungi, are sold in great quantities in late summer and autumn.

In the interests of speed and economy, Monpazier houses would originally have been built of wood and, despite precautions, they were eventually destroyed in battle or by fire. The stone houses that replaced them bear the marks of successive epochs and styles. A mullioned small-paned window of the fifteenth century, for instance, might have a decorative eighteenth-century balcony added, and dormer windows may now emerge from roofs which were once plain.

Mosset, Pyrénées-Orientales

In early spring the pretty terraced houses of Mosset contemplate a view of flowering cistus bushes. The grand Pyrenean outline of the Pic du Canigou is some ten miles to the south and a little further beyond is Spain. The Pyrenees do not form the massive mountain barrier between the two countries that a quick glance at the topographical map suggests. The natural lie of the land is of valleys running north and south; geographically the Basque country and Catalonia have a foot in each country, and this is reflected in mutual influences of architecture and a way of life. Mosset is just north of Prades, which was the adoptive home of the Spanish cellist Pablo Casals who exiled himself here in 1939 after the Spanish Civil War.

Mostuéjouls, Aveyron

Mostuéjouls sits astride the River Trébans just before it loses itself in the River Tarn. Over millions of years the Tarn has eroded a magnificent gorge through the vast limestone plateaux of the Causse de Sauveterre to the north of the village and the Causse de Méjean to the south, its luminous jade-green water flowing over a white gravelly riverbed beneath sheer tall cliffs. This landscape conceals a network of underground watercourses which have developed where water seeping through the porous limestone meets a layer of impermeable rock. The water, which follows gravitational pull, is joined by other streams and falls in cascades, creating galleries and caverns within the rock, and eventually, invisibly, feeds the Tarn through a system of underground rivers. Sometimes, however, the water reappears at the earth's surface in a powerful stream and joins the Tarn overground.

Moustiers-Sainte-Marie, Alpes-de-Haute-Provence

Slung between the two horns of rock behind Moustiers is a gold star on an iron chain. It is called the *cadeno* and legend says that when a baron of Blacas was freed from captivity with King Louis IX (Saint Louis) during the Seventh Crusade, he returned to Moustiers to fulfil a vow he had made while he was in prison. To hang the star was his votive gift, and there it still remains, renowned throughout Provence.

Rushing out between the gaunt shoulders of the cliffs behind the village comes the torrent that is the cause of this dramatic rock formation. It tumbles through the village beneath a canopy of undergrowth and fig trees and under several bridges, effectively splitting the village in two, then runs away to join the River Maire before both streams are finally engulfed in the heart-stoppingly sinister Grand Cañon du Verdon.

Beyond Moustiers with its flowering alleys and pretty lanes, the road winds up the side of the mountain to the fifth-century chapel of Notre-Dame-de-Beauvoir, fragile against the rock face. Bodies of still-born children were brought to the chapel for baptism and even now, every September, it is a place of pilgrimage. As you approach the chapel you pass exquisite modern examples of the faience for which Moustiers is famous. In the seventeenth century the pale-blue- and buff-coloured glazes came from Faenza in Italy, but gradually the Moustiers potters put their own stamp on the craft and nowadays an authentic piece of early Moustiers faience is a collector's item.

Najac, Aveyron

The houses immediately below the château of Najac were once soldiers' billets. The rest of the village creeps Indian file along the crest of a ridge which plunges vertiginously away to the river. The walls of the houses are either timber-framed or of undressed stone and mortar made with sand from the riverbed, but the lintels and uprights to doorways and windows are always of plain or simply decorated dressed stone. None of the houses has a cellar for they are built on tough old granite cliffs. Towards the river are a number of little two-storey pigeon houses; for want of cow manure in these parts it was pigeon dung that served as fertilizer.

Of all Aveyron villages it is Najac, with its striking position above the river, that most keenly evokes the drama of its past. The first fortress to be built at the height of this rocky loop in the gorge was erected by Bertrand de St-Gille, Count of Toulouse, in about 1110. When Najac joined the Albigensian heretics in the late twelfth century, it was from this perfect military standpoint that they hoped to defend themselves against the Crusaders. But Simon de Montfort, whose brief from Pope Innocent III was to put down the Cathar rebellion at any price, led his army against the fortress and destroyed it and probably all of its valorous defenders. It was rebuilt in 1253 by a brother of Louis IX, and a plain and sober Gothic church was built nearby.

Naves, Ardèche

Below the dizzy heights of the Barre range of hills, Naves looks over the fertile basin of the River Chassezac where chestnut and mulberry trees pad out the lower slopes in lumpy green upholstery. The mulberry trees are a reminder of the once thriving silk-worm industry. From its beginnings in 1536, through to the invention of mechanical looms in the nineteenth century, silk-worm farming provided the *paysans* – which should be taken to mean countrymen not peasants – with the major part of their income.

Most houses in these villages possessed a *clède*, a building for storing and drying chestnuts. Even today, chestnuts are a main constituent of the winter diet, especially for bachelor farmers living alone with no inclination to cook; while the cows are milked or the vegetables hoed, a saucepan of chestnuts can simmer for hours and never seem to overcook.

Noyers, Yonne

Sixteen towers preside over the battlements that encircle Noyers (pronounced Noyère), which neatly fills a meander in the River Serein and thus doubles its defences. The smart side of the village, inside the curve of the river, is a lesson in the architectural styles of four centuries: pretty mullioned windows of the Renaissance, tall steep roofs of Louis XIV and the tidy tailored stonework of the eighteenth century are set off by the much earlier, half-timbered corbelled houses of the Middle Ages.

Noyers, Yonne

It is a short walk in Noyers from the obvious wealth of the houses in the Place de l'Hôtel de Ville to the poorer quarter, where the houses belonged to small-scale wine growers or *vignerons*. The cellar doors are at street level and an outside stairway leads you to the main entrance on the first floor. Some of the houses still have their old *lauzes* roof, and the immense weight of the limestone slabs forced builders to construct triangular arches over doors and windows to distribute the load.

The street names of Noyers give a glimpse of the village's past importance and of the activity and bustle that filled the narrow alleys and squares from dawn till dusk: Rue du Poids-du-Roy, Place du Marché-au-Blé, Place du Grenier-à-Sel and the inviting Place de la Petite-Etape-aux-Vins.

Ornans, Doubs

Ornans, south of Besançon in the Franche-Comté, is the birthplace of the painter Gustave Courbet (1819–77). In the oldest part of town the houses back straight on to the River Loue which in spring, swollen with meltwater from the Jura, rushes through the town in a magnificent milky froth.

The River Loue laps against the walls of the house where Courbet was born and which is now a museum. The rugged valley to the west of Ornans was one of Courbet's chief inspirations: of his great genre paintings, *Enterrement à Ornans* is the best known, but the robust and earthy pastoral scenes of *Le Château d'Ornans* and *Source de la Loue* remind you of this still little known but most engaging part of France.

Peillon, Alpes-Maritimes

From well below Peillon you can see the village like an eagle's eyrie on top of a thick stump of rock. It is a perfect medieval hill-top village, the constraints of the site governing its shape but also providing the one essential, a defendable position. Many of the mountain-top villages above the Mediterranean coast grew from the time of the earliest Germanic invaders of the fifth and sixth centuries who, taking the low routes inland, drove the villagers from the fertile valleys into the mountains.

Centuries of continuous attack saw little change in the growth of Peillon or in the lifestyles of its inhabitants: it was only in the nineteenth century that Peillon built a village fountain, and even this water was carefully rationed during the summer months. The houses expand upwards following the contours of the rock face and become more spacious at each level. A stable cut into the rock would have a communal room above it, then one or two bedrooms and a hayloft under the roof. Outside, stairways and vaulted alleys rather than streets lead you from house to house.

Pérouges, Ain

In the late nineteenth century, the little village of Pérouges was very nearly demolished. The movement of people away from rural life to the big industrial centres and the security of a steady job left villages like Pérouges empty and deserted. But just in time, a group of artists, writers and others clubbed together to buy, restore and re-inhabit the old houses and to preserve them as a perfect example of a medieval village.

The village of Pérouges, with its new facelift, is unnaturally immaculate, but it is far preferable to losing the village altogether. Half-timbered, corbelled houses stand shoulder to hip with graceful Renaissance dwellings, slim towers and a stocky Romanesque church. It was from the church that the villagers defended their lives during a damaging but not disastrous siege in 1486, when the duchies of Savoy and Dauphiné both claimed the village as their own.

Pérouges, Ain

Having withstood a siege in 1486, the villagers of Pérouges rebuilt the damaged houses with a mixture of earth and river stones called *galets* in varying proportion, and gave them overhanging roofs to protect the more friable walls from the rain. *Galets* pave the streets, including the Rue des Rondes, named after the rounds the nightwatchmen diligently tramped out.

Rieux Volvestre, Haute-Garonne

Rieux is an excellent example of how brick, timber and stone can be used together to present a decorative yet functional whole. Even houses with the simplest arrangement of building materials will have lintels, doorposts and cornerstones of dressed stone, their haphazard size softening any possible austerity. The houses of notables have façades which are distinctly fanciful, with bricks arranged in a herringbone pattern or set out like a chessboard between timber frames. Rieux, for long a humble farming village, suddenly bounced into respectability when Pope John XXII promoted it to *cité episcopale* in 1317. The presence of the new bishop brought inevitable social and political reforms. The townsfolk found new wealth and built defending walls to protect it and themselves, but after four hundred years the bishopric was dissolved and Rieux returned to its quiet agricultural existence.

121

Rochefort-en-Terre, Morbihan

The village of Rochefort-en-Terre lies in romantic countryside in one of the secret parts of Brittany some way from the coast. The village houses bristle along the top of a granite ridge, but the land falls away on every side to deep grassy dells and streams, miniature stone-walled orchards and sudden dark ravines. It is a part of Brittany that has bewitched painters and writers in search of solitude and perhaps even melancholy.

Rochefort originated as a medieval fortress and developed over three centuries into a prosperous community with its own law courts and elegant main street of sixteenth-century houses. In emulation of its name, the land is wrapped around the village like a mantle. At the first sign of spring, the old balconies explode into colour with geraniums and pansies, while hydrangeas, mimosa and climbing roses fill the streets. The church, with its elaborate porch and four flamboyant gables, was founded in the twelfth century. It is called Notre-Dame-de-la-Tronchaye and it takes its name from a statue of the Virgin Mary found stuffed into a hollow tree during the Norman invasions. An annual pilgrimage venerating the statue takes place in August.

Roussillon, Vaucluse

Roux means 'rust-coloured', and Roussillon, as its name suggests, is the ochre village. It stands on a great vertical outcrop of rich brown rock, surrounded by a frilly green collar of pines. This is where in the nineteenth century, France's ochre quarries vied for importance with the bauxite mines to the west, but they diminished as chemical dyes made their appearance. Ochre, which is a mixture of sandy clay and iron oxide, is placed in running water where the sand is separated and the remaining ochre-clay mixture is then dried, cut into blocks and ground into powder. It is used as paint pigment, especially in the building industry.

At the height of the ochre-quarrying period, Roussillon itself nearly disappeared under the quarryman's pickaxe, since it stands on the richest deposit of ochre in the area. Fortunately, the little Romanesque church and belfry surrounded by the engagingly rosy village houses were left untouched. The main ochre quarries are now some way beyond the village.

For three days at Ascension-tide the village streets are filled with the activity and sounds of the ochre festival. According to legend, when Raymond d'Avignon, who owned these lands, discovered that his wife had fallen in love with his page, he killed the page and served his heart on a platter to his wife. In her anguish she leapt off a cliff and a spring gushed out where she fell. Her blood is said to have coloured all the surrounding countryside.

Rudelle, Lot

You could be forgiven for imagining that the church of Rudelle with its crenellated parapet and arrow slits was really a fine feudal keep. The instability that was the hallmark of south-west France in the thirteenth and fourteenth centuries led to the fortification of many of its churches, providing refuge for the villagers from pillaging bands of soldiers. The sombre block of Rudelle was built in the thirteenth century by Bertrand de Cardaillac, the seigneur of Lacapelle-Marival. Lying on the busy high-road between Rocamadour and Figeac, pilgrims passed through Rudelle regularly on their way to Santiago de Compostela, and with them travelled bands of footloose soldiers and mercenaries. It was a foolhardy traveller who chose not to stop at Rudelle or neighbouring Thémines during the hours of darkness. From the terrace of the church you can peer through the machicolations and contemplate the effect of dropping stones or pouring molten lead onto your enemies below.

Slate tiles on the roof of this unusually elegant little house are much less common than the flat red tiles on the barn and outbuildings. Barns are almost always built into the slope of the land, and if no natural slope exists a manmade one will be constructed. Carts and ploughs are dragged up the grassy ramp and stored inside with the hay, while the animals are driven into the stables below through a large square side door on the lower level. In many cases, a Périgord barn is infinitely more handsome than the house to which it belongs.

Saignon, Vaucluse

Saignon possesses a Romanesque church and ruined fortress and is perched on a promontory overlooking the Apt basin. It is one of many villages that barely escaped total destruction when François I determined to quell the members of a religious sect who were known as the Vaudois. Their founder, the fundamentalist Peter Valdo, was excommunicated in 1179 for having the bible translated into Provençal, and his followers fled to the safety of secure villages such as Saignon. In 1332 there began one of the most vicious and bloody campaigns in Provence's history against these so-called heretics. They were imprisoned, tortured, burnt, and whole villages were razed to the ground. They were blamed for bad weather, disease, poor crops and were either starved or burnt out of their mountain hideouts when watercourses were blocked and whole hillsides set alight. Survivors fled to Switzerland and settled in the area known today as the Vaud Alps.

Saint-Bertrand-de-Comminges, Haute-Garonne

Below the rocky hump where the village now stands are the ruins of a much earlier and more substantial Roman provincial capital city, where Herod Antipas, tetrarch of Galilee, was exiled with his wife by Caligula shortly after the Crucifixion. The Garonne and its fertile banks are close by, and it is easy to imagine the tramp of Pompey's legions arriving here on their way to or from Spain, barely two days' march away. The Roman city was virtually destroyed by barbarians in the fourth century, and in the sixth century plague struck. Only a handful of houses remained, sheltering under the hill, until in 1120 Bertrand, bishop of the county of Comminges, built a cathedral here and a new community developed. It is a remarkable building, with a cloister open to the valley on one side where the view of fields and meadows, vines and cypresses is an integral part of this place of worship.

Saint-Cirq-Lapopie, Lot

St-Cirq (the 'q' is silent) takes its name from the third-century saint St Cyr, and from Lapopie, the seigneur who built a fortress here in 1110. The village stands above the River Lot, clamped like Rocamadour to the side of the limestone cliffs. It was once a busy little village whose walls hummed to the rhythm of wood-turners' lathes: the cask taps made here from local maple were in demand all over France. Now, the village has only 150 inhabitants and their incomes derive from tourism, such has been the effect of mechanization on small independent communities. Fortunately for St-Cirq it is arguably the most beautiful village in France. From the fourteenth-century church at the height of the cliff the houses tumble downhill in a wonderful chaos of terracotta roofs, creamy stone walls, ancient timber and narrow shadowy streets so steep people used to take their shoes off to get a better grip on the cobbles.

If you look up to the roofs and balconies that nearly meet above your head at St-Cirq, you will see the sign of the Auberge des Mariniers du Lot, where boatmen put up after a day's hard hauling on the river. Until barely a century ago, the Dordogne and Lot rivers still played an essential part in the commercial life of the region. Upstream from the coast they carried supplies and information, and back down on purpose-built rafts went timber, stone, ores and – the most intriguing cargo of all – juniper berries for the Dutch gin trade.

Saint-Cirq-Lapopie, Lot

Medieval builders were not deterred by awkward terrain; nor could they afford to be in these parts. If there was no room for a village to grow along a riverbank, then upwards it must go. St-Cirq's vertical hold on the rock face also proved a useful defence against aggressors for in spite of, or perhaps because of, its unassailable site, it was frequently under siege, especially during the Hundred Years War. But it was the Huguenot Henry of Navarre who finally demolished the fortress in 1580 and with it St-Cirq's strategic value. The fortified church remains, however, and its robust walls, watchtower and air of vigilance are reminders of St-Cirq's military past.

Saint-Cyprien, Dordogne

St-Cyprien lies in the Périgord Noir, where the River Dordogne runs through alluvial meadows and fields of wheat and tobacco, past the châteaux of Castelnaud and Beynac, until the upland forests and limestone cliffs that edge the river flatten out into the vineyards of Bordeaux. Above St-Cyprien stand the ruins of Fage castle which was burnt down by German soldiers in their hunt for Resistance workers. Below the village is the Renaissance château of Les Mirandes, once lived in by the American singer Josephine Baker.

The abbey church of St-Cyprien presides over the compact little village. Built in the twelfth century, it was much restored when Romanesque architecture flowered into Gothic. A little way north of St-Cyprien are the caves of Les Eyzies, spectacular not just because they reveal the vast stretches of labyrinthine architecture beneath your feet in the limestone, but also because of their prehistoric wall-paintings.

Sainte-Enimie, Lozère

The village of Ste-Enimie lies at the bottom of a tight fold in the Tarn gorge towered over by sparsely wooded limestone cliffs. The medieval houses cling to any available ledge above the river, high enough, the builders must have hoped, to be safe from flood water. They are roofed in flattish silvery stones of schist called *lauzes*, quarried further up river on Mt Lozère.

The steep and narrow streets of Ste-Enimie are studded with exquisitely rounded stones gathered from the bed of the Tarn. A little way above the village and seeming to spring from the rock itself, stands the Romanesque chapterhouse of a nunnery founded in the sixth century by Enimie, a daughter of one of the long-haired Merovingian priest-kings. According to legend, Enimie wished to devote herself to God, and when her brother, King Dagobert, insisted that she marry she became afflicted with a terrible leprosy. In a vision she was ordered to seek a miraculous spring which would restore her to health. Travelling for days, she eventually discovered the spring in a wild and remote valley, bathed in it and was cured. But when she tried to leave her leprosy returned. Again she bathed, was cured, and again as she left she became a leper. Believing this to be a sign from God, she spent the rest of her life in this place, founded an abbey and was canonized.

Sainte-Enimie, Lozère

In the tiny squares with their pollarded trees and vines, and behind the thick walls of the houses, you will find workshops where artisans make their living out of basketry, woodcarving, and weaving the rough wool of the *causses*.

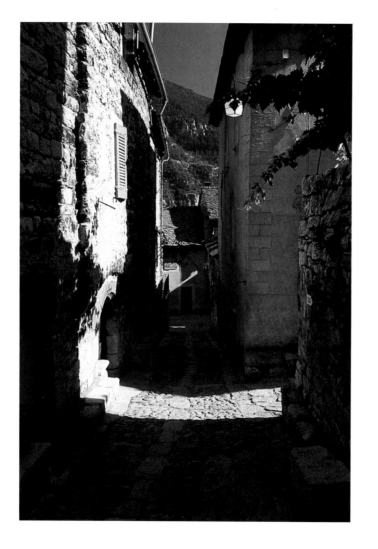

Saint-Guilhem-le-Désert, Hérault

St-Guilhem became a gathering place for pilgrims on their way to Santiago de Compostela. The body of Guilhem, Duke of Aquitaine and Prince of Orange, was buried in the abbey church when he died here in 812, and later the village took his name. Guilhem had been one of Charlemagne's childhood friends and later became his closest and staunchest lieutenant. Tragically all that is left of the abbey Guilhem founded is the church and a quiet square pool in the cloisters, the last of the gardens he designed. The cloister of the abbey is not complete itself because most of it was dismantled and sold to the United States, where it can now be admired in the Cloisters Museum in New York.

Saint-Guilhem-le-Désert, Hérault

The clean and simple
Mediterranean lines of
St-Guilhem-le-Désert are a
curious contrast to the grim walls
of the Verdus gorge at its back.
The village used to be called
Gellone (the abbey is still known
by that name), but after Guilhem
lived and died here and was
canonized the village was
renamed in his honour. It is said
that a Saracen giant who
terrorized the land lived on a
rocky cliff above the village and
that Guilhem's last heroic act was
to kill him in single combat. On
Good Friday the faithful walk in
procession through the streets,
each person carrying a tiny
oil-lamp made from a snail's
shell.

The Abbaye de Gellone was founded in about AD 760 by Guilhem. Charlemagne's priceless gift in recognition of Guilhem's services was a piece of the True Cross, about three inches long, which Charlemagne himself had received on a visit to Rome. Guilhem's much-loved wife died when he was not yet fifty, and it was then that he decided to go into retreat, choosing Gellone as an ideal, isolated spot to build an abbey.

Saint-Médard-de-Presque, Lot

In the shadow of her more illustrious sisters Autoire and Loubressac, St-Médard gives the impression of being in deep slumber all day long, as if time and progress have passed her by. If you sit in the dusty little square and watch the day pass, you will probably observe the daily round of village life: herds of cows lumber through the square to be put to graze; the women bend over their vegetable plots; and old men play *boules* in the sun while their dogs pant under plane trees.

The great castle beyond St-Médard is Castelnau, an eleventh-century keep of red ironstone, surrounded by later massive fortifications. Wherever you are in this valley, your eye is irresistibly drawn to this magnificent stronghold which once garrisoned 1,500 men.

Saint-Privat-d'Allier, Haute-Loire

Like many of the medieval villages in the southern half of France, St-Privat was fortified against the bands of soldiers which wandered about the countryside in search of booty both during and after the Hundred Years War. The Romanesque church, with its simple tower and belfry, formed part of the fortifications built into the side of the hill. Over the years, the village has crept discreetly down below its ramparts to take advantage of the natural terraces in the land before it drops away to the Allier gorge. Minute vegetable gardens display the green-fingered talent of the French countryman. It is quite usual, too, to find a bright clump of marigolds marking the end of a line of cabbages, or hollyhocks standing by a row of maize.

Salers, Cantal

It is said that the famous mahogany-red cattle of Salers that graze all summer long on these grassy uplands, lose the fiery tint in their coats if they change to lower pastures. True or false, the high *planèzes* of Cantal are immensely fertile. Cantal itself is one giant extinct volcano which once had several active craters. The lava from these has decomposed and enriched the soil, producing some of the best pastures in France.

Salers is a grim-faced little town at first sight, especially on a wet autumn day when the walls of volcanic stone and grey dismal roofs can look gloomy and forbidding. But the impression is short-lived. Salers is one of the least spoilt villages of the fifteenth and sixteenth centuries, straddling medieval and Renaissance styles, and displaying a wealth in its houses and small châteaux that is still supported today by the continuing success of the Salers cattle. Modest houses in the village were built with ungraded rough-cut blocks of black stone and held together with thick dollops of white limey mortar. Where the mortar squeezed out of the cracks it was smoothed over the stone and in some cases an entire wall has been covered with it. The roof-tiles are *lauzes*, thin slices of schist that twinkle in the sun in a distinctive fish-scale pattern. In winter, when Salers is invariably snow-bound, the effect of the dark walls and shining roofs is remarkable.

Salers, Cantal

The wide windows often seen on the houses of Salers are later additions or enlargements of the original small ones. Builders in the early Renaissance were still influenced by military architecture more akin to medieval times, when all openings were small and therefore less vulnerable. After the Hundred Years War was officially over, isolated places like Salers were justifiably nervous of the aimless bands of soldiers who had nothing better to do than pillage and loot. But military architecture had other more lasting effects. For example, the little watchtowers you sometimes see pinned to the corner of a house were built to accommodate not watchmen, but spiral stairways leading to the upper storeys, thus creating more space inside.

Séguret, Vaucluse

Séguret, wrapped round the base of a steep rocky hillock, is a charming collection of stone houses and interlacing squares and streets. The village square, usually with a fountain and often a *lavoir*, or washing place, has always been an essential meeting place, much more so than the English village green. In the hot climate of southern France, much spare time would be spent outside the house simply sitting and gossiping in the company of neighbours.

Séguret, Vaucluse

The women at the *lavoir* would have used a paste of wood ash to bleach their linen, which was then rinsed and hung between the houses to dry in the sun. Until well into this century the village fountain and *lavoir* were probably the nearest sources of fresh running water. Nowadays, the *lavoir* is occasionally used to wash bulky sheep fleeces before they are made into mattresses or blankets.

Semur-en-Auxois, Côte-d'Or

Inside a meander in the River Armançon rises a table of pink granite rock on which stands Semur's redoubtable set of ramparts and, beyond them, the grey walls of Notre-Dame cathedral. The ramparts reinforced the original fourteenth-century citadel of Semur, inside which was the so-called dungeon flanked by four enormous towers. One of these is now cracked from top to bottom and no longer has its original crenellations. It is called the Tour de l'Orle d'Or and its name, meaning 'golden hem', derives from the distinctive coppered lead which once covered its battlemented roof. The ensemble of fortifications made Semur the strongest town in Auxois. Small houses, some gracious others quite humble, have tucked themselves into the available cracks and terraces over the years, all embellishing the view of Semur as you approach it from the west.

Semur-en-Auxois, Côte-d'Or

The oldest inhabited and most built-up quarter of Semur surrounds the cathedral of Notre-Dame, which was founded in the eleventh century and altered periodically until well into the sixteenth century. The walls of the houses are of soft grey stone, the steeply sweeping red roofs cover spacious attics which were the servants' quarters. By comparison, in the less densely populated but much poorer south, servants slept and ate in the same room as their masters until the First World War. Houses of the wealthy *bourgeoisie* are often in a privileged position shoulder to shoulder with the church.

The excellent soil and mild climate of this part of Burgundy have meant that food has never been scarce, and relatively few people have experienced that terrible poverty familiar to villagers in the south. Cattle from the great white Charolais breed provide beef, while milk is produced by the black-and-white Montbéliarde cattle, native to Auxois. In the countryside around the village and further south grow the vines which produce Burgundy's famous wines.

Vézelay, Yonne

Vézelay crowns a great sweep of Morvan countryside. At the highest point of the village is its jewel, the abbey of St Mary Magdalene where Mary's remains are believed to be buried in a column shaft in the south transept. In Vézelay in 1146 St Bernard, abbot of the cistercian monastery of Clairvaux and the most influential theologian of his generation, called upon Christians to fight the Second Crusade, in the presence of Louis VII and his courtiers. From this time, Vézelay became the point of departure for one of the four main pilgrimage routes to Santiago de Compostela. In 1190, King Philippe Auguste and Richard the Lionheart met here before leaving on the Third Crusade, and in about 1217 St Francis founded the first provincial French order of Friars Minor.

The streets of Vézelay, now calm except in high summer, were in the Middle Ages crammed with thousands of excited pilgrims. Its church rang to the sound of priests exhorting sacrifice of personal goods and devotion, its inns were bursting with the less austere pilgrims who could afford to pay for shelter and a bed, while others flocked to the great, partly underground, chambers near the abbey built specifically to house the itinerant crowds. These evocative caverns with their vaulted ceilings and great fireplaces can still be seen. In between the grand departures, which were accompanied by fairs and markets, the people of Vézelay returned to their more humble pursuits, tilling the land, sowing, reaping and tending vines.

Vézelay, Yonne

The cloisters of the abbey were built in about 1190, at the same time as the new choir which had been destroyed in a terrible fire in 1120. A thousand pilgrims who had come to pray before the relics of Mary Magdalene were burnt to death. Then came the discovery of other supposed relics of the same saint in Provence in the town of St Maximin. Doubt set in, and gradually there were fewer fairs at Vézelay, fewer markets and fewer pilgrims. The wars of religion, the Huguenots and finally the Revolution made Vézelay a crumbling ruin. The plight of the village first came to the attention of the government in the early nineteenth century, and the young architect Viollet-le-Duc was employed to restore the abbey, a task that took him nineteen years to complete.

Vieille-Brioude, Haute-Loire

In the Haute-Loire some forty kilometres south of Clermont-Ferrand, the busy village of Vieille-Brioude presides over this part of the Allier valley and the plentiful supply of salmon that swims up the river each spring. In the oldest part of the village, the basilica of St Julien is a fine example of the fusion of Romanesque architecture and Auvergnat craftsmanship. Inside, the warmth of the reddish sandstone fills the nave with striking colour.

The River Allier waters the excellent soil which has made Brioude and other villages in the valley into prosperous centres of agriculture. The earth is almost black, rich with decomposed lava and volcanic ash tipped into the river valleys during volcanic activity sixty million years ago.

Collonges-la-Rouge, Corrèze

The wide stone arch with its expertly graded and matched blocks of red sandstone once accommodated stout double doors of oak or chestnut, through which passed cattle and farm vehicles into the stable or courtyard beyond. The doors have been adapted to provide light to the living quarters which now replace the stable.

Photographic Notes

Photographing villages in France can present far greater problems than photographing English villages. The French village street is often no more than eight feet wide and can have houses three or more storeys high on either side. In high summer, sunlight can penetrate these narrow streets only in the middle of the day and in winter the sun might not reach the street at all. Keeping the home cool in summer is a major consideration in the design of many village houses all over France and the village has often developed in such a way that each house can successfully shade its neighbour. The centre of a village can therefore often be broken up by heavy blocks of shadow and photography can prove difficult. Using a polarizing filter can help to enrich the sky but it also removes much of the reflection and detail that exist within shadows. I had to use graduated filters sparingly as they can really only be effectively used when there are no buildings or trees protruding into the area where the under exposure takes place. I certainly feel that such a filter is most successful when its use is not apparent.

Weather conditions in France seem to be more changeable even than those in England. As I am fond of theatrical lighting I often find that it is worthwhile waiting for an hour or so observing the sky waiting for the right conditions. It is possible with patience to 'place' light with the help of fast-moving clouds to reveal or conceal various areas. A fair wind can be useful in this respect although for long exposures it can be a hindrance.

I have used the 81 series of filters for many of the photographs within the book together with various lenses from 24mm to 300mm. In most cases I used either Kodachrome 25 or 64 film because in my view their resolution is undisputed. Most exposures were made using the time-delay facility on the camera as opposed to a cable release to ensure minimum vibration.

People and cars always present a problem to any photographer and patience is required waiting for conditions when their presence is not obtrusive. I have also tried to avoid as far as possible manmade obstructions such as telephone wires. French villages in midsummer are bustling with activity and extremely popular with tourists, and the restrictive light conditions and human activity of the summer months can make the photographer's task a hard one.

Sainte-Enimie, Lozère

The flourishing vine growing against a sunlit wall is in a sense as much a part of the house's structure as the stones and tiles. The dense shade it provides when the sun is high keeps the kitchen cool and dark even when the street door is open.

Bibliography

Cocula-Vaillières, A.-M. *Une Fleuve et les Hommes*, Editions Tallendier

Deschamps, Marion *Portrait of Brittany*, Robert Hale, 1980

Duby, Georges and Mandrou, Robert *A History of French Civilization*, Weidenfeld and Nicolson 1964; USA, Random House, 1975

Goubert, Pierre *The Ancien Régime*, Weidenfeld and Nicolson, 1973; USA, Harper and Row, 1970

Goubert, Pierre *French Peasantry in the Seventeenth Century*, Cambridge University Press, 1982; USA, Cambridge University Press, 1986

Gutton, J.-P. *La Sociabilité Villageoise dans l'Ancienne France*, Hachette, 1979

Keen, Maurice *The Pelican History of Medieval Europe*, Penguin, 1968

Le Roy Ladurie, Emmanuel *Montaillou*, Gallimard, 1975

Le Roy Ladurie, Emmanuel and Morineau, Michel *Histoire Economique et Sociale de la France* (Tome I, Vol. II), Presses Universitaires de France, 1977

Longnon, Jean and Gazelles, Raymond (Introduction) *Les Très Riches Heures du Duc de Berry*, Thames and Hudson, 1969; USA, Abrams, 1984

Michelin Green Guides to France

Maurois, André *A History of France*, Cape, 1949

Oyler, Philip *Sons of the Generous Earth*, Hodder and Stoughton, 1963

Les Plus Beaux Villages de France, Reader's Digest, 1977

Sol, Chanoine E. *Le Vieux Quercy* (2 Vols), Bibliothèque de la Maison des Oeuvres

Tuchman, Barbara *A Distant Mirror*, USA, Alfred A. Knopf, 1978

White, Freda *Three Rivers of France*, Faber, 1952

Wylie, Laurence *A Village in the Vaucluse*, Harrap, 1961; USA, Havard University Press, 1957

Index